MW00633659

AGILE & RESILIENT:
SALES LEADERSHIP
FOR THE NEW NORMAL

Agile & Resilient: Sales Leadership for the New Normal

Copyright © 2022 by The Brooks Group.

All rights reserved.

No part of this book may be used or reproduced in any manner whatsoever without written permission except in the case of brief quotations embodied in critical articles and reviews.

For more information, address:

The Brooks Group
310 North Elm Street
Suite 900
Greensboro, NC 27401, USA.

ISBN 978-0-578-36476-6

Acknowledgments

This book would not be possible without our clients—the sales organizations we've had the privilege of working with throughout the years (especially in the 2020s). We've learned from every one of them, and the concepts we present here reflect those experiences.

Corrie Lisk-Hurst, our editor and advisor, guided two rookie authors through the writing process. Draft after draft (and month after month), she helped us focus our message and bring our ideas to life.

Lauren Davis, our project manager, kept us on task and on time. We appreciated the "gentle reminders" of approaching deadlines and her coordination of the many moving pieces involved in producing a book.

The Brooks Group's Creative Team—Ellie Russell, Emily Strader, and Rachel Jones—made us look good with an eye-catching cover design, layout, and graphics. They handled every edit with a smile and a positive attitude.

The Leadership Team and our colleagues at The Brooks Group gave us the time and space to write this book. Their encouragement was inspiring, and we are grateful for their confidence in the finished product.

And finally, we thank our spouses (Eric Richardson and Julie Sharer) and our families for their enthusiasm at our idea to write a book and their patience and support while we *wrote* it.

Foreward

"Sooner or later, something fundamental in your business world will change."

Almost 30 years ago, Andy Grove, the then-CEO of Intel, wrote those words as he reflected on a near-death experience of his company precipitated by what he later named a "strategic inflection point."

As a first mover in the memory chip industry, Intel had practically 100% of the market it had built since its founding in 1969. By the early 1980s, the ground had begun to shift beneath them.

Japanese competitors were gradually and remorselessly making inroads into Intel's leadership with high-quality, low-priced, mass-produced parts. It was imperceptible at first, but by 1985 Intel was in serious trouble. Finally, after an extended period of denial "wandering in the valley of death" and hemorrhaging money, the company decided to do the unthinkable and exit the business it helped to create.

The decision was made to focus on what was then a niche business—microprocessors to serve the emerging personal computer industry. The executive team met with entrenched resistance internally. Intel, and its culture, were defined by what it made—memory chips.

The sales team, in particular, could not let go of the belief that they needed a "full product line" to do a good job in front of customers.

It was a wrenching change of direction, but Intel survived and flourished by taking painful and radical action.

In his book *Only the Paranoid Survive*, Grove chronicles his strategy of focusing on a new way of measuring the nightmare moment every leader dreads—moments he refers to as "strategic inflection points"—when massive change occurs and a company must, virtually overnight, adapt or fall by the wayside. Corporate giants such as Kodak, Nokia, and Blackberry failed to heed the lesson of Intel, even though it was written on the proverbial wall in large letters. They either did not to see the signs or, more likely, chose to rationalize them away until what they made faded into irrelevance.

According to Grove, an inflection point is reached when the old strategic picture dissolves and gives way to the new view of the world, and the future begins to look significantly different than the past. It's at such points that business leaders and managers realize: Things are different. Something has changed.

It's safe to say the entire world has just experienced such an inflection point.

While it's become something of a truism that the global COVID pandemic simply accelerated trends that were already in place, fundamental aspects of life have changed. Things really are different. A lot has changed.

The perfect storm created by a combination of the pandemic, enforced national lockdowns, and the availability of digital technologies that made it possible for businesses to react, readjust, survive, and often flourish in a radically altered global environment has changed fundamental aspects of life, perhaps permanently.

Technology has given people liberating options. Many are rethinking how they live their lives. A global pandemic without apparent end has provided workers with the impetus to evaluate their careers, long-term goals, and working conditions. The Great Resignation (the word economists have coined for the extraordinary employee exodus from work) is a reflection of the deep dissatisfaction with previous work/life situations.

Technology is also transforming industries and institutions—education online, health care through telemedicine, robotic surgery, or home health monitoring. The "Amazonification" of commerce—already well under way before the pandemic—has changed people's buying habits and their service expectations. Delivery tomorrow, or even today, is the new norm. Sophisticated B2B and B2C e-commerce platforms have helped to create a new era of small business entrepreneurs.

According to a study by McKinsey, the management consultancy, what started out as a crisis response has now become the next normal, and it has profound implications for how buyers and sellers will do business in the future.

For example, both B2B buyers and sellers say they prefer the new digital reality, and more than three quarters say they now prefer digital self-serve and remote human engagement over face-to-face interactions—a sentiment that has steadily solidified, even after lockdowns ended.

Self-serve and remote interactions have made it easier for buyers to get information, place orders, and arrange service, and customers are enjoying the speed and convenience. Only about 20 percent of B2B buyers say they hope to return to in-person sales, even in sectors where field-sales models have traditionally dominated, such as pharma and medical products.

B2B sales leaders have moved from an initial reluctance to adopt digital in reaction to the widespread shutdowns in the early stages of the pandemic to a growing conviction that digital is the way to go.

And B2B customers are buying online in a big way. A significant indicator that digital sales have come of age is the comfort B2B buyers have in making large new purchases and reorders online. The prevailing wisdom was that e-commerce was mainly for smaller-ticket items and fast-moving parts. Not so anymore. Notably, 70 percent of B2B decision makers say they are open to making new, fully self-serve, or remote purchases in excess of $50,000, and 27 percent would spend more than $500,000.

Globally, B2B decision makers say that online and remote selling are as effective as in-person engagement, or even more so—and they're not just talking about selling to warm leads. Sellers also believe digital prospecting is as effective as in-person meetings to connect with existing customers.

With the massive shift to digital, video and live chat have emerged as the predominant channels for interacting and closing sales with B2B customers, while in-person meetings and related sales activities have dropped precipitously.

The study goes on to say that e-commerce and videoconferencing now account for 43 percent of all B2B revenue, more than any other channel. Customers also made it clear that, given the choice, they prefer video to phone.

Significantly, survey respondents believe these pandemic-induced patterns are likely to become permanent. Almost nine in ten decision makers say that new commercial and go-to-market sales practices will be a fixture.

The book you are holding builds on each of these trends, providing context, ideas, and tools for leaders who want to make their sales organizations more agile and resilient for the market conditions ahead.

As with Intel all those years ago, something fundamental in your business world has just changed. What a tremendous opportunity.

Alan Brew
Founding Partner, BrandingBusiness
www.brandingbusiness.com

TABLE OF CONTENTS

Introduction

This is not the book we expected to write when we started ideation in early 2020. It is fair to say that a global pandemic changed our plans! While COVID interrupted or paused many aspects of selling, we observed that it also demanded that certain changes accelerate in the most agile and resilient sales organizations.

It is absolutely clear: Sales leadership as usual just will not work any longer. At The Brooks Group, we have been training and coaching business-to-business salespeople and sales leaders for more than 40 years. Throughout that time, we have seen a steady group of core fundamentals as critical to success—prospect intelligently and consistently, prepare to have quality sales calls, ask good questions to understand what really motivates buyers, and connect the dots between what buyers need and want and what you offer as a supplier. Selling fads and quirky approaches have come and gone, but the fundamentals—what our founder Bill Brooks called IMPACT Selling—have consistently been the way to improve results.

That said, starting late in the twenty-teens, as the makeup of typical B2B sales forces and the technologies used in their day-to-day work were changing, we started to see the best sales organizations add some important things to our list of selling fundamentals. Intentional sales cultures, team alignment, understanding of buyer journeys, and useful metrics were just a few of the areas the best of the best sales teams used to stay ahead of the competition.

Then 2020 happened. Walking day-by-day with our clients through the start, middle, and now (we hope) the end of the pandemic has helped us see very clearly that, to quote Marshall Goldsmith, "What got you here won't get you there."*

Today's B2B customers are very clear that they see little value in most sales calls. Buyers have wrestled control of the buying process away from sellers, seeking contact and content only after they have short-listed options and built an evaluation model, including a low, cost-based price.

At the same time, sales leaders tell us their teams are not properly preparing for calls, talking more than listening in sales calls, and too often leading with price.

If any of these issues sound familiar to you, please read on. Through research examples, client conversations, and our own experience, we describe six key trends making their impact on sales organizations today. We have also worked hard to provide implementable ideas and resources that will help you lead where you need to go. Not sure where, exactly, you need to head? Reading this book is a good first step.

We encourage your thoughts and feedback on this book and hope you will share them with us at contact@thebrooksgroup.com.

Michelle Richardson
Russ Sharer
February 2022

Chapter

1

The Only Constant Is Change

Sellers get fired all of the time.

Your customers find "better prices." Your production line has quality issues. Someone else can source it faster. Or even more painful? Your sales team broke trust with the buyer by being slow to respond (or not responding at all), making that customer angry for no good reason.

However, we think the toughest reason to be fired as a supplier has to do with getting out-innovated. Russ tells several stories in training programs to bring this point home:

> A paper goods supplier saw a China-based competitor enter the market with a large catalog, next-day delivery, and low prices. Local paper distributors—the supplier's core distribution channel—couldn't compete and started going out of business. Guess what happened to the supplier's distribution business?

> Conversely, a semiconductor company came up with the idea of creating bonded cages to store products within their customers' factories. The material belonged to the supplier, but when it was needed, the cage was opened, units removed, and the customer charged. This change required a bit of investment, but it completely removed time wasted due to excessive demand for components. Guess whose competitors were at a competitive disadvantage?

> A forward-thinking medical device company created a risk-sharing program, wherein if a device they had sold to a hospital experienced any issues over a designated period of time, the manufacturer shared with the hospital the costs associated with replacement. Guess who loved this arrangement...and continued to buy a higher per unit device?

Each of these is an example of how one company innovated, better addressing the real need of their customers, and through that gaining a competitive advantage in their market, enabling larger sales, increases in gross margin, and/or stronger customer relationships. Even if someone in their organization said, "Well, that's never been done," or, "That's outside our product line," or, "That's just not how we do things," they persisted and changed.

They grew their business, and their competitors always paid a price.

It is our premise that the decade of the 2020s will demand companies continually improve their innovation and problem-solving capabilities, addressing areas truly valued by their customers. We saw it through the COVID pandemic, and there is nothing to think this demand for continually rethinking and improving the buyer/seller relationship will change any time soon. In fact, we think it will accelerate.

Change-Makers Are Big Winners

Each of those top-performing companies *caused* positive change in their industry, customers' businesses, supply chain, or processes instead of just *responding* to change (though some of them did fantastically well at responding to change, too). You know it is an old adage because it is true: Change is the only constant in the world. As sales professionals, we will always have a need to navigate changes skillfully and intelligently in ways that benefit our companies and our clients.

All three of the companies we just described illustrate core capacities that always have been essential for high-performing sales organizations and likely will continue to be well into the future.

- **They focused on delivering quality products and services.** Buyers will always want assurances from your salespeople that the product or service they are going to buy from your company is of good quality for the price they pay.
- **They were responsive to their customers.** Customers will always expect a quick response to their calls, emails, texts, and direct messages. That is

true whether they reach out to your salesperson, customer service, tech support, or you as a sales leader.

- **They listened.** People will always want to be listened to and heard. This is simple human nature, and salespeople who listen carefully and understand where buyers are in their buying journey usually get the sales results they need.

- **They looked for ways to make life easier for their customers, to address their real problems, needs, and wants.** Successful salespeople know that customers will always want the solutions they buy to make their own lives easier (not just their company's—their own).

- **They were agile.** Companies will always need to be flexible and adaptable when faced with change, and salespeople must be a driving force in anticipating and adapting to change.

While each of these capacities is timeless, the way goal-crushing sales professionals are practicing them to benefit their customers adapts in response to changes in the economy, political approaches, market shifts, technological advances, off-shoring or on-shoring of manufacturing, and supply chain patterns.

Adapting to Change Is a Condition of Staying in Business

From organisms to organizations, those that are able to adapt to change are the ones that survive and thrive. There were many businesses that survived the Great Depression of the 1930s, plenty that survived the Recession of 2008, and countless that responded well to rapid change during the COVID-19 pandemic. Think about Costco and Target, who rapidly embraced home delivery, parking lot pickup, and a shift to more "at home" products from their supply chains. Or on the business side, look at Office Depot, which quickly extended corporate buying agreements to provide equipment necessary for work at home. Microsoft frequently innovated its Teams product to make it easier to use and a better fit for distributed virtual meetings. Many B2B companies sent their workforces home, yet kept on delivering results. Many companies thrived in spite of (or perhaps because of) the pandemic—many companies not only survived it, they grew through it.

In 1982, Tom Peters and Robert H. Waterman, Jr., wrote *In Search of Excellence*, exploring the management approaches and organizational effectiveness of many large companies. This book was *the* management reference guide for nearly 20 years, and for good reason: Of the 43 public companies described in the book, 32 "substantially outperformed the Dow Jones Industrial Average and the broader S&P 500" at least initially.[1] But interestingly, over the 20 years from the book's publication, the "great companies" were just as likely to perform badly as well. According to a *MarketWatch* analysis, the companies' odds of outperforming the market were only 52–48, just slightly better than a coin toss.[2] In addition, six of the companies were out of business before 2000.

Challenges = Opportunity

Thirty-one percent of organizations that characterize themselves as "highly agile" have increased EBITDA by 20% or more. In contrast, only 1% of organizations that characterize themselves as having "average agility" have gained as much.[3]

Most companies want to be more agile, but 59% don't have the cultural attributes—ranging from willingness to share knowledge to quick decision-making—that are fundamental to agility.[4]

Only 43% of HR professionals say their organizations can "quickly turn challenges into opportunities." Less than a third say their organizations have a learning and development strategy that helps leaders at all levels to be more agile.[5]

Eighty-five percent of the jobs that will exist in 2030 haven't been invented yet.[6]

Jim Collins's classic management book, Good to Great, *was published in 2001. Of the 11 companies described in that book, one is now out of business (A&P) and several were acquired. Companies on the* Good to Great *list also ended up embroiled in some of the biggest scandals of the last ten years: Wells Fargo, Fannie Mae, and Philip Morris.*

Degree of Sales Organizations' Change Implemented Since COVID

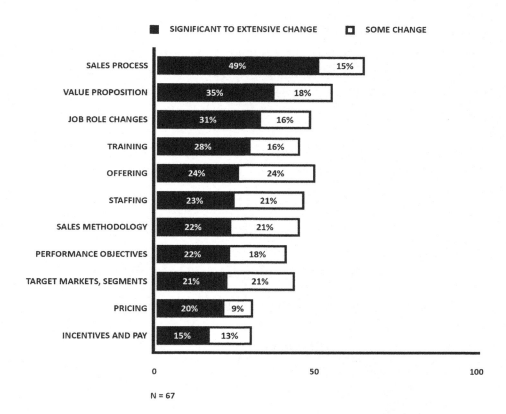

Percentage of Firms

■ SIGNIFICANT TO EXTENSIVE CHANGE   □ SOME CHANGE

- SALES PROCESS: 49% | 15%
- VALUE PROPOSITION: 35% | 18%
- JOB ROLE CHANGES: 31% | 16%
- TRAINING: 28% | 16%
- OFFERING: 24% | 24%
- STAFFING: 23% | 21%
- SALES METHODOLOGY: 22% | 21%
- PERFORMANCE OBJECTIVES: 22% | 18%
- TARGET MARKETS, SEGMENTS: 21% | 21%
- PRICING: 20% | 9%
- INCENTIVES AND PAY: 15% | 13%

0   50   100

N = 67

We hear the message loud and clear: A company that cannot change effectively can go from excellent or great to average or out of business fast. The ones that succeed change. Period.

So What's Changed in Sales?

The Sales Management Association (SMA) did some research around the impact of the pandemic on sales strategy in late 2020, looking at roughly 67 firms.[7] Fifty-two percent of the organizations that they surveyed had experienced "significant to extreme" impacts on their sales organization; another 28% experienced some level of change. Only 20% reported "little to no change." So, a significant majority of those surveyed reported changes in response to the pandemic.

To us, that is not really a surprise—we have been noticing changes in sales organizations for many years. We will say again and again in this book that *the pandemic accelerated the need for changes that already were in process and/or needed to be initiated.* What is pretty interesting to us at The Brooks Group is the top five areas that organizations in this study made changes to—all of which are topics you will find we talk, write, and train about regularly:

1. Sales process
2. Value proposition
3. Job role changes
4. Training
5. Offering

Degree of Overall Change Implemented Since COVID
Percentage Distribution of Firms

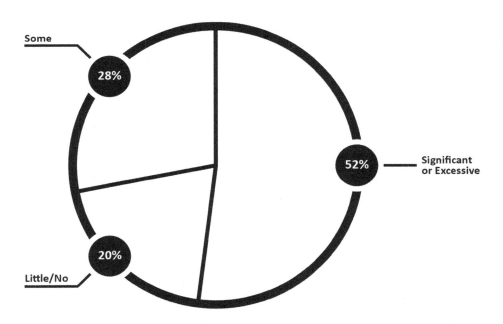

Compare the top to the bottom of the chart: incentives and pay, pricing, and target markets and segments were among the areas where the least change has been made. Do we think those were the right choices? Does it vary depending on industry? How will we know if they are the right choices?

Some of these changes were obvious and forced upon companies; for example, if they had been utilizing an in-person sales process, they had to change. If they had been primarily prospecting via events, that too had to change. But other shifts were more subtle, driven by refocusing the business into its most successful or value-contributing areas. Some of the strongest companies looked at the various sales team members in early 2020 and asked, "How can you be most effective right now?"

Some of our clients refocused senior people on existing accounts, making sure that they were serviced well during 2020. Others shifted similarly experienced people to business development roles, asking them to start conversations with new customers whose businesses were doing well in the pandemic and whose existing supply chains might be troublesome. Still other clients trimmed or grew their product offerings based on customer requests and needs. One client—a building supply distributor—sought ways to add products that could increase the average revenue per order to increase profitability on each delivery. If the trucks were running, how could they contribute more revenue and margin per trip?

In early 2020, many people had never heard of Zoom, yet a few months later the phrase, "You're on mute!" was being repeated thousands of times a day. Training on virtual skills—how to host better meetings, how to properly light your home office, even what the best ways were to present—became "must know" skills. Many sales leaders used the time saved from travel to refresh selling skills for their teams.

Every business looked at an unprecedented event and asked, "How do we succeed now?" Those who adapted lived to fight another day. Those who couldn't adapt didn't have to answer the question, "When do we go back to the office?" because the office was shuttered.

There's no question the speed and degree of change that has been necessary for every organization has been astonishing. Whether organizations have made the right choices in what changes to make for the long haul is yet to be seen; in the shorter term, the surveyed companies reported moderate effectiveness in the changes they have made.

The TOPO Research (now Gartner) *Sales Leadership Report 2020* revealed similar trends—among top strategies identified by sales leaders were: value-based selling, strong sales culture, well-executed sales processes, and other strategies that seem consistent with those reported by the SMA. If you are reading that list and thinking, "But aren't those all just common sense?" Yes. Yes, they are. But "common" sense is not as common as one would think. While just about everyone says these are what is required to succeed, the vast majority fail to execute change.

None of the organizations surveyed by the SMA had more than 50% effectiveness in successfully implementing changes. We do not have a lot of data on this yet, but our guess is that there are likely too many partial adherents. Too many leaders talk change, but do not invest the time into coaching. Rather, they stress "get the deal" and reward results, even if achieved in a non-scalable way. (We are going to help show you how to avoid that problem throughout the rest of this book.)

Not surprisingly, the most adaptable organizations outperform their peers: The organizations that rated themselves as most effective in implementing change have projected performance over the next 12 months that is much higher than their peers who reported less effective change management.

Change-Driver #1: Buyers Are More Sophisticated

One of the most significant changes sales organizations are dealing with is the systematic transformation of how corporate buyers approach their purchasing decisions. We have all watched how Amazon has transformed the direct-to-consumer marketplace. It did not put every brick-and-mortar store out of business, but far too many ignored the threat, saying, "But doesn't Amazon sell books? They can't sell what I sell." (Of course, now Amazon does just that!) Those that have survived and thrived did it by adapting and staying clear about their own value proposition.

The B2B universe has been a few steps behind individual consumers, but business people are also consumers, their expectations continue to be reshaped, and they are now demanding the same levels of transparency, responsiveness, and self-service from their business suppliers as they have come to expect from the places they purchase consumer goods. As Forrester Research reported in late 2020, "B2B Selling Approaches Lag Buyer Expectations and New Realities."[8]

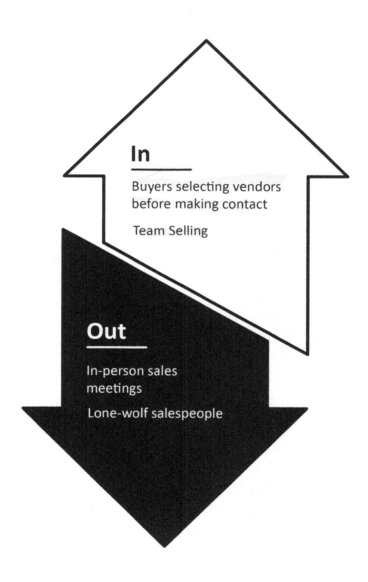

In

Buyers selecting vendors before making contact

Team Selling

Out

In-person sales meetings

Lone-wolf salespeople

Buyers: In the general sense, individuals involved in making purchasing decisions (equivalent of "consumers" in the B2C world).

Customers/Clients: Individuals or companies who are currently engaged with your company.

CxO: An individual at the executive level of an organization, with a title like CEO, CFO, COO, CIO, CMO, etc. (Sometimes collectively referred to as C-level or C-suite).

Procurement: Though used interchangeably with "purchasing," procurement refers to a more strategic role responsible for identifying needs, sourcing suppliers, negotiation and contract management, and spotting opportunities for cost-savings.

Prospects: Individuals or companies who have either (a) not ever purchased a product or service from your organization, or (b) may have purchased from you previously, but are prospective customers for a new or different product than they have previously bought.

Purchasing: Typically, individuals or a department tasked with ordering goods and services.

Buyers today are:

- clear about what is and is not critical to their business,
- frustrated with vendors overpromising and underdelivering,
- facing supply chain issues (and frequently looking at onshoring),
- able to seek pricing alternatives easily, and
- demanding to buy direct rather than through distribution, expecting manufacturers to perform the functions of many distribution channels at little to no cost, managing stocks of inventory and making quick shipments.

Many, if not most, corporate buyers are building a "short list" of vendors before they ever make any contact with a vendor's sales organization. There are many peer-to-peer vendor comparison sites, such as G2, Clutch, PeerInsights, and others, that help buyers make connections with suppliers— LinkedIn groups, Google, Alibaba, and others. Information that is available online and through their personal professional networks lets them narrow the potential supplier list, saving them the time and annoyance of bad meetings with too many unqualified prospective suppliers.

This buyer behavior is well-researched:

- Seventy-seven percent of B2B buyers don't talk to a salesperson until they have done their own research.[9]
- Ninety-nine percent of B2B buyers are comfortable spending $50K or more making a purchase entirely through a digital self-service model.[10]
- B2B buyers only spend 17% of the buying process meeting with potential suppliers.[11]

Change-Driver #2: Digitalization Is Here to Stay

Clearly, Internet research has risen to the top of buyers' "go to" approaches. A McKinsey study of approximately 3,600 decision makers globally explored what B2B customers want, and how they think about their businesses differently after the events of 2020.[12] Some of the key findings that jumped out at us were as follows:

- The desire to have digital interactions has doubled; mobile app ordering has grown more than 250%.
- The importance of the buyer's digital experience doubled.
- Sixty-five percent of these decision makers are saying that remote selling is equal to or more effective than the "old way."

There is ample evidence that even generations who perhaps are not as used to interacting digitally have gotten more comfortable with it over time. Add these folks to those younger generations who have grown up with technology seemingly attached to their hands, and it is clear that industry was moving toward digital channels before COVID. COVID just accelerated the journey, and it is here to stay. Virtual selling is now as important as prospecting, in terms of being a critical success skill for salespeople.

We have confirmed the same in our research. Before COVID, when we surveyed sales leaders about their ratio of in-person to virtual selling, the average response was 80% in-person to 20% virtual. More recently, in mid-2021, we asked the same question, and the response was 55% in-person to 45% virtual. Yet too many B2B suppliers still have only minimally embraced digitalization, thinking relationships will continue to be the driving factor for buying. They are falling behind.

Change-Driver #3: Transparency Is Expected

According to Merriam-Webster, *transparency* is "the quality that makes something obvious or easy to understand," and *transparent* means, "able to see through; easy to notice or understand; honest and open: not secretive."

For our purposes, let us describe it this way: Transparency is achieved when a customer has information into your revenue operations and supply chain so they can make better decisions—and, simultaneously, your internal team has the same information to effectively service customer requests. (We will delve more into transparency in a moment.)

Digitalization also means information is expected at any time of the week or day. Questions that today's B2B buyers demand to have instant or near-instant answers to include:

- Does the supplier I'm considering manufacture or resell the product I need?
- What is the status of my P.O.?
- How many units are in stock?
- Is it too late to get it on the truck for delivery in the morning?
- Can I order units after 6:00 p.m.?
- What is a realistic expectation of when we will receive back-ordered product?
- What is it like to work with the consulting firm I am considering engaging?

In August 2021, COVID closed China's Ningbo-Zhoushan port, the world's third-largest container port and China's biggest port for furniture, home goods, toys, and auto parts.[13] At the time, reports projected it could take a month or more to return to normal operations. If you were a buyer for a major online marketplace or retailer, the second you heard about this closure you knew instantly that this could affect your Christmas inventories and sales. You either had—or in the next 24 hours demanded—transparency from your suppliers.

How Am I Affected?

Transparency is not just about inventory and other post-sale questions. The kind of transparency buyers want enables them to get the answer to, "Am I affected?" in a few minutes or hours, not days. Buyers want real-time, truthful insights—often before they commit to a purchase from you. Transparency looks like:

- **Honesty:** It is not just about in-stock or out-of-stock, but capabilities. Does the product or service perform in the way I require it to perform? Or will I be surprised later?
- **Clarity:** From a pricing perspective, does the price include all shipping or freight costs? Is there anything bundled or hidden in the investment?
- **Realistic Risk Assessment:** How reliable is the supply chain? What fail-safes are in place to ensure I will not be left high and dry?
- **Communication:** What is the real value a seller adds? Are they communicating at the essential touch points your clients expect? (If your products are commodities, this is especially important, but it is no less true for highly specialized services or rare products.)

You will have to determine what that transparency looks like to your markets and customers. To some, it is 24/7 telephone support manned with knowledgeable product and application experts. To others, it is private online portals where a customer can track the delivery of orders in real-time. And still to others, it is an ERP system that immediately pushes notifications on product delays to the buyer—and alerts sales to reach out proactively to discuss options. Or maybe it is extensive training for your customer service representatives so they can immediately recommend a compatible alternate for the out-of-stock item.

If your company operates under a "get the order, then worry about the delivery" mindset, chances are your customers will increasingly give you this order: "Get out. I'm not interested." A better approach is working diligently to ensure your company and every customer touch point with your organization is seen as value-adding to their business and them, personally, as B2B buyers.

Change-Driver #4: Buyers Often Want to Avoid You, No Matter How Much "Thought Leadership" You Bring

For many years, salespeople and their companies have sought to become "thought leaders," writing and publishing case studies, white papers, application notes, articles, and much more. Buyers wanted to make better decisions, and vendors sought to educate them through these means. But when a methodology is overused, it loses its effectiveness.

A simple Google search of "thought leadership" today returns nearly 600 million articles. For years, it has been a truism that thought leadership is the key to positioning, and it is absolutely still a key to sales success. Being a smart partner for your prospects and customers gets real results. By making the most of their connections and expertise within their own and related industries, sales professionals can find many ways to make themselves indispensable to their customers. But emailing white papers is no longer unique. Everyone has been doing that for years, and most companies have archives of white papers, blog posts, research reports, case studies, and more—at the click of a button on their websites and social media feeds.

Not surprisingly then, a report from saleshacker.com showed recently that 72% of buyers first search for solutions on Google once they are aware they have a business problem to solve.[14] With face-to-face meetings in person reduced, your online presence—both in terms of thought leadership and detailed content about your offerings—needs to be powerful enough to attract and hold buyers' attention. The catch is that YOUR information must add clarity to the buyer, not contribute to their sense of being overwhelmed or confused by conflicting information.

Buyers often want to avoid you.

In 2017—well before the pandemic—a Gartner study reported that B2B buyers spend 62% of their time in buying learning independently online and offline.[15] They will do everything they can to make their way to a purchase decision without involving a salesperson.

Some of this is because there *is* excellent information out there in easily accessible formats, and buyers *can* find a lot of the details they need on their own: In fact, 54% of younger buyers want to make purchase decisions entirely digitally, with no direct human contact.[16] That is why your company's online presence must be strong.

At the same time, we are seeing that corporate risk-aversion since the Recession of 2008 has made a variety of CxOs get more involved in purchase decisions. This makes for an interesting situation: Buying teams or groups that include C-level decision makers who typically do not have time for details and a lot of information. Some of that is related to responsibilities of the position versus how they are wired. An important consideration here is that CxOs tend to view purchase decisions through a different lens than other types of buyers (we will talk more about this idea later in the book when we introduce our Decision Making Pyramid).

The implication for sellers is that they need to communicate at the right level and address the underlying motivations of these C-suite buyers. But on the buying side, more people—with different perspectives and motivations (plus a lot of overwhelming information)—mean more difficulty reaching decision consensus. Sales professionals need to be able to connect the dots for everyone on the committee—even if the CxO carries the most weight.

In B2B sales, there is a tremendous amount of opportunity for adding value in the sales process if you are aligned with your buyers' journey. Your company's digital materials are only part of that picture. When prospects and customers recognize that your sales team and your solutions bring real value to their operations, you are much more likely to win initial sales and get repeat business. And guiding buyers through the purchase decision process with collaboration and trust is a significant part of the value your sellers offer.

Salespeople need to become experts at guiding a buyer through their purchasing journey. Your sales team must help your prospects and customers see a clear path through an information overload in every step of the sale—

connecting them with resources, clarifying complex information and processes, and collaborating with them to arrive at solutions. That ultimately gives them confidence that you are trustworthy and knowledgeable and, therefore, more likely to turn to you first the next time they need to make a purchase.

So, What is Ahead?

McKinsey & Company predicted in May 2021 that "catastrophic events will grow more frequent but less predictable. They will unfold faster, but in more varied ways. The digital and technological revolution, climate change, and geopolitical uncertainty will all play major roles."[17] The pandemic of 2020–21 showed clearly that the impacts of surprise catastrophic events are far-reaching and deeply felt. We can see that those companies that have survived and thrived are ready to take on what is next, served well by the blend of resiliency, creativity, and intelligence that got them through the pandemic.

We refer to companies in trouble—those that do not have a clear strategy toward product focus and corresponding profitability—as "zombies," dead but still walking: They sell undifferentiated copycat products that offer no real unique value when compared to their competitors. These firms consistently struggle to be profitable and do not have the financing, staffing, or focus to reinvest in new designs. There is an often-cited anecdote that

> *McKinsey & Company predicted in May 2021 that "catastrophic events will grow more frequent but less predictable."*

Jack Welch, when he took over at GE, demanded that companies in the GE portfolio be #1 or #2 in their markets or get out.[18] Clearly, he recognized that market share and profitability are intricately related.

In 2019, Apple shipped less than 25% of the total smartphone market and was actually number two in the market that year—with a market capitalization of more than $1.1 trillion. Apple does not have the biggest volume, but they took in more than 60% of the total profit-share of the industry by focusing on high-value products and the consumers who choose them.

Today, people point to Apple as the company they would most like to beat, yet it was not that long ago that Apple was building unexciting computers, seeing new products fail (anyone remember Newton?), and its long-term viability was in question. In fact, in 1997, Michael Dell said, "[If I were put in charge of Apple], I'd shut it down and give the money back to the shareholders."[19] Then Steve Jobs returned, focused the product line, created differentiated new lines of business (iPod, iPhone, iMac), and launched Apple 2.0. It is still reaping the benefits.

And while we have mixed sales and corporate stories so far in this chapter, our passion is helping sales leaders and their salespeople recognize the need for change and guide them through it. Sales does not stand still. Imagine you are a salesperson with a multi-city territory in 1921. Your boss calls and says they are no longer going to provide you a company horse, but they are offering you a company car. What is your reaction? How long will you be able to keep your job if you say, "No, thanks. I know how to take care of my horse. Feed is easier to find than gasoline. I have a good relationship with my horse." What happens when your peers can serve their customers more quickly and cover more territory in their cars, while you are trotting along on Lucky?

It is no different now. One of our company leaders at The Brooks Group tells a story in training that exemplifies this:

> *I went to work for a Telecom equipment start-up that was focused on serving a very specific customer set. A month after joining the company, there was a major shift in the market and the original target customers—competitive telephone carriers—not only stopped buying equipment, but also started going out of business. In the course of two weeks, the company changed target customers, refocused their sales efforts, and were able to thrive while other Telecom equipment providers crashed and burned (both startups and longstanding players). Those two agile weeks saved the company.*

During the pandemic of 2020–21, as strange as it may seem to some of us, there were salespeople who refused to make necessary changes. We heard people confidently assert that things would "go back to normal" soon, and they would return to cross-country travel, dropping in on potential customers, and face-to-face customer visits. However, the sales professionals

I was successful by be a Zoom consultant

who have thrived (and let's be honest, in some industries surviving has really been the only possible outcome) are those who have adapted quickly to digital and hybrid selling models. These are people we will describe later in this book as hybrid sellers. In some cases, these were folks who had been seeing the trends and had already changed their selling approach pre-pandemic. In others, companies or individuals realized that they *had* to make changes if they hoped to stay relevant as professionals in their business.

Are You Muscled Up and Ready to Play?

Between 1966 and 2021, 55 years of changes happened in and to the PGA. The basic game of golf is the same—you start at the tee, you keep the ball in the fairway, you put it on the green, then you make the putt, and you get the score—but a lot of the game has changed as well. In 1966, Jack Nicklaus was 26 years old, golfing with persimmon woods. He was in his career about five years, won three tournaments, and made a grand total of $111,000. Now look at Bryson DeChambeau: In 2019, he was 26 and had been in his career about five years. He won once and had five top-ten finishes in tournaments—and made $3.2 million. Talk about an increase in efficiency per transaction over the years!

But here is something important to note. Think about the average golfer's fitness level when Jack Nicklaus went on the tour. When he was winning, he was not the trimmest athlete; in fact, golfers were perceived not to be "real athletes" then. Today, due to players such as Tiger Woods, and especially now, DeChambeau, golfers are training like other athletes. DeChambeau has muscled up, gotten in fantastic shape, and rebuilt his game. In the last two years alone, he has won three tournaments, finished in the top ten 18 times, and won $12.1 million.

All of this is a great analogy for us as sales professionals. We have to ask ourselves if we are in great shape. Have we changed and muscled up our approach to sales during our careers? The average amateur golfer around the world spends just over $200 per year on equipment, looking for whatever will give them that edge. We strongly encourage you to think about selling not just *now*, but tomorrow and next year. We believe we cannot increment our way to success—that is going to be too slow—so we are going to have to place some bets.

Key Takeaways from This Chapter

- **Change is the only constant.** The decade of the 2020s will demand companies continually improve their innovation and problem-solving capabilities, addressing areas their customers truly value.

- **Change-makers are the big winners.** Top-performing companies *cause* positive change in their industry, customers' businesses, supply chain, or processes instead of just *responding* to changes (though some do fantastically well at responding to changes, too).

- **Too many people talk change but do not execute.** That goes for sales leaders who talk change but do not invest time in coaching their team *and* for individual salespeople who focus on quota even when they know focusing on what buyers need and want is the pathway to the sales results for which they are aiming.

- **Four change-drivers:**

  1. **Buyers are more sophisticated than ever.** A systematic transformation of how corporate buyers approach their purchasing decisions in recent years demands that sales professionals transform how they approach selling.

  2. **Digitalization is here to stay.** While a majority of decision makers believe remote selling is equal to or better than in-person sales, too many B2B suppliers still have only minimally embraced digitalization, thinking relationships will continue to be the driving factor for buying. They are falling behind.

  3. **Transparency is expected.** Transparency is achieved when a customer has information into your revenue operations and supply chain so they can make better decisions—and, simultaneously, your internal team has the same information to effectively service customer requests.

  4. **Buyers often want to avoid you, no matter how much "thought leadership" you bring.** Salespeople must become experts at guiding a buyer through their purchasing journey, helping them see a clear path through an information overload in every step of the sale—connecting them with resources, clarifying complex information and processes, and collaborating with them to arrive at solutions.

Ask Yourself

- What has my team done right in anticipating or responding to changes brought about by the COVID pandemic and other factors in recent years?
- How is the buyer/seller relationship changing in our industry?
- How am I coaching my team to anticipate and adapt to change in our business?
- What does transparency look like to our customers?
- Am I "muscled up and ready to play?" Have I invested in my own knowledge, skills, and capacities?

Looking Ahead

In the rest of this book, we will be delving into research (our own and others'), client stories, and, yes, *thought leadership* about how to lead your sales team in an era of unprecedented, rapid change. The following is a quick snapshot of what is ahead:

- In Chapter 2, we will talk about how B2C buying has transformed how B2B purchase decisions are made and introduce the six key changes we predict will continue to impact B2B sales.
- In Chapter 3, we will explore the importance of paying attention to how buyers look for information and manage the buying process and decisions within it and introduce the concept of the successful hybrid seller.
- In Chapter 4, we will take a close look at how culture (even more than compensation) can empower your sales team, encouraging sales behaviors that get results—or cost you your most successful people.
- In Chapter 5, we will look at the KPIs and other measures of success that will help you respond to and anticipate the continuing changes that the sales industry will face.
- In Chapter 6, we will focus on the essential importance of agility in sales organizations, particularly when confronted with the increasingly common team buying dynamic, meeting buyers where they want to be met.

- In Chapter 7, we will explore how to maintain margin through a strong value focus and empowered negotiation in the face of aggressive price competition and buyers pushing hard for a low price.
- In Chapter 8, we will explore how strategic planning and a deep awareness of buyers' wants and needs allows your salespeople to personalize sales interactions.
- In Chapter 9, we will paint a picture of today's top sales professional, who is able to connect with buyers effectively to create the personalized experience their buyers demand.
- In Chapter 10, we will sum it all up and give you a practical checklist of to-dos for this week and six months from now.

CHAPTER 1 FREE TOOL
Your Sales Team's Competitive Advantage Analysis

https://brooksgroup.com/download-tools/

Chapter

2

How B2C Buying Has Transformed B2B Selling

Transition gas, hybrid, to ev.

In countless white papers, blog posts, articles and essays, tweets, and interviews, sales experts have predicted the death of the sales profession as we know it. They point to statistics that reveal buyers are involving salespeople later and later in the buying process—if at all. They lament the fact that organizations are restructuring and reducing the size of their sales forces and putting all their budgeted dollars into Internet marketing.

While those observations are, no doubt, at least partly true, we have a more optimistic view of our profession. Of course, things have changed. Of course, some of the changes have been difficult to swallow. The last time the world faced such a dramatic shift in "the way things work" was probably between the mid-1990s and mid-2000s, when the Internet became a key part of virtually everyone's lives.

But here's the thing: The sales organizations and sales professionals who had already positioned themselves as value-adding resources to their customers have, by and large, survived the upheavals of 2020 and 2021. (We are calling these folks hybrid sellers.) And if they have been consistently agile and ready for change, they have likely thrived. Let us take a look at why this is the case.

In the absence of a value interpreter, every product or service essentially becomes the same. When buyers can access mountains of details, comparisons, and price data online, any time, day or night, your product or service can look just the same as your competitor's. It may even look less valuable or more expensive. However, if you can reduce risk and/or help a customer innovate, you have built unique value for your business and for your customer.

We have a client that distributes building supplies, and many of its brands are the same as those offered by competitive distributors. One of its salespeople noticed that one of their contractor customers was employing two people full time to remove scrap from a multistory office tower under construction. The salesperson offered an innovative solution, first recommending that rather than buy bulk product and have it cut on the site, the contractor could buy prefabricated product that eliminated waste. Second, the salesperson offered to deliver the product not just to the site, but to the floor on which it was to be installed.

The net result? The contractor saved money on the project, the two laborers could be redeployed to more significant tasks, and our client received a higher margin on the project, even when extra delivery effort was factored in. The salesperson's innovative thinking showed a desire to add value to serve the customer and an agility to rethink solutions for a win-win result.

To bring innovative solutions, a salesperson needs to engage the potential customer earlier in the buyer's journey, sometimes even before the potential customer has identified a need or decided to buy. While not necessarily in the example just mentioned, it is likely further savings and benefits could have been accrued if our client had been involved even earlier—in the design and bid of the contract. The phrase "value engineering" too often means cutting the cost of the project, but innovative companies are figuring out how to use it to add value—to the customer and to their products/services.

Yet despite the variety and depth of changes that have taken place and continue to unfold in the B2B sales profession, many of the fundamentals have stayed the same.

Quality Is Still the Boss (With a Few Caveats)

As you no doubt have realized, salespeople do not have control over their product or service quality. Sure, you can share customer feedback with the plant manager or R&D, or quality assurance, or your manager, or even your bartender. However, you are not the one tasked with maintaining the quality of your company's offerings. That said, though, it *is* incumbent on you as a salesperson to really understand your buyers' quality expectations so that you can deliver the appropriate solutions to them.

We did a survey of B2B procurement professionals not too long ago, seeking to understand the factors that influenced their buying decisions. We wanted to see what strategies they used to negotiate, what behaviors they would like to see more from salespeople, and what activities and attributes could tip the scales away from "lowest price" in their buying decision. Far and away, the number one answer was "quality." Perhaps not surprisingly, the more closely aligned the decision maker is with the long-term use of a product, or the more their company's reputation is tied to it, the more they are concerned about quality.

> One of our clients relayed a story of a site visit ahead of submitting a response to an RFP for flooring for a commercial office building. A competitor won the business five years ago, and now the customer was looking to replace the flooring. During the walkthrough, the facilities manager pointed to some flooring installed in an office and said, "That flooring is only five years old," to which the incumbent salesperson said, "Yep, looks pretty good for five years," and continued walking.
>
> In contrast, our client's salesperson looked at the flooring and asked, "How long do you want the flooring to last?" The facilities manager said they just signed a seven-year lease and wanted the flooring to last the length of the lease. Recognizing the focus of the RFP, our client's salesperson said, "I can provide flooring for seven or more years, but not out of the RFP you have released. I would love the chance to talk about lengthening the floor's life, and why the RFP will not deliver that kind of product before you make any final decisions."
>
> They met the next day, the RFP was cancelled, and our client got the business. Quality and value won above a lower priced solution.

But there are a couple of interesting things to note about quality.

Quality Is Not Necessarily a 100% Objective Measure

On a production line, quality might refer to something like conformance to specific metrics, appearance standards, or other specifications. In sales, we recognize that quality does not just include objective measurements such as those, but *also* more subjective ones, especially if you are selling services.

We define quality the following way:

Quality = Performance, or the ability to meet required specifications.

Interestingly, "required specifications" can vary widely.

Think about Harbor Freight Tools. Although they give their products strong brand names, such as Warrior, Chicago Strong, Hercules, and Pittsburgh Forge; in reality, their users see them as disposable, purchased at a low price with the expectation they will have a very short life. Sometimes the tool does not even last through its first use, and they just keep fingers crossed that it will not break down on a critical project. The prices are so low, the performance requirements are significantly below those of quality branded tools.

In contrast, consider one of The Brooks Group's clients, an eyeglasses frame distributor that is not a famous, well-known name brand. They strategically sell frames only to optometry and ophthalmology practices, partnering to provide doctors with a high-quality, stylish selection of frames that cannot be price-shopped at big box stores or online. This means added revenue to their clients' practices. Before a doctor endorses a product, they want to be sure it is of a quality that is worthy of the trust their patients place in them. They could stock their practices with cheaper frames, but that would not match the quality of experience the doctors seek to ensure their patients enjoy. By selecting high-quality eyeglasses frames, the distributor's clients are presenting their patients with differentiated products that, while they may be slightly more expensive than some competitors, will provide a long-term positive experience that matches the perception of quality they get from their eye doctor.

What do B2B buyers think? Fifty-nine percent of respondents on a recent survey told us that performance to expectations would justify a higher price. They defined that performance as meeting their specifications and performing as promised.

So...

Quality = Performance = Value for the Cost

When you understand what the customer values, and you present your solution in a way that clearly highlights how you deliver that value, you are able to sell at better margin. In our basic IMPACT Selling training programs, every participant learns what we call the Value Formula:

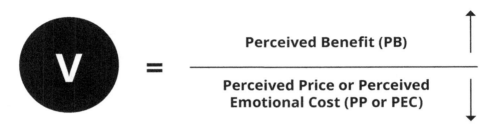

We will delve deeper into this formula in a later chapter, but for now, notice that value equals perceived benefits over perceived price and perceived emotional cost. Here is how it works. Your client sees *value* if he or she believes that the benefits they will receive from purchasing your product or service outweigh what they will pay for it (price) and any difficulties with terms, conditions, transition, learning curve, installation, etc. (perceived emotional costs).

Here's an interesting example:

> *One of our building supply distribution clients purposefully hires most of its salespeople from the trades—these salespeople used to install the products they now sell. So, when someone purchases the company's products, these experienced technical salespeople can value-add, making sure the materials list is complete, ensuring the right type of material is used, or suggesting qualifying alternatives if the initial item is unavailable, for example.*

In this case, "quality" does not just mean the products themselves are well made, easy to install, and reliable. It means they are all those things, *plus* the buying experience is a quality one because buyers believe the information they are getting from the company's salespeople has value. They are willing to pay a higher purchase price for the products because working with our client ends up saving them on overall project costs.

Quality equals performance to anticipated standards *and* value for the cost. The smartest sales professionals and most successful sales organizations know what matters most to their customers and prospects. They see the role of sales as a trusted advisor, assisting buyers to reach the solutions that do not just match whatever technical specifications are required, but also guiding them through the process from awareness through consideration to purchase and beyond.

Positioning and Pre-Call Preparation Are Non-Negotiables

It is not enough to be friendly with the person to whom you are attempting to sell; pretty much any sales professional worth their salt knows that by now. It is a time-tested principle that you must be seen as a trusted resource for your buyers. Nowadays, that means offering what Gartner describes as "extreme value" at every possible interaction

> *Quality = Performance, or the ability to meet required specifications.*

with them.[20] They describe extreme value as "offering insight and experiences to help a buyer address mission-critical priorities," which may look like the following at each step of the buyer's journey:

- **Awareness of Need:** You may provide your point of view on nuanced market shifts in their industry.
- **Consideration of Options:** You might help buyers—whether prospects or existing customers—have experiences that explore how their peers are thinking about similar priorities.
- **Purchase:** You work to design and propose solutions specifically targeted to align with their mission-critical priorities.
- **Customer Support:** You help them navigate the change management process (if necessary), offering support during installation, deployment, etc.

Sales Should Add Value Throughout the Buyer's Journey

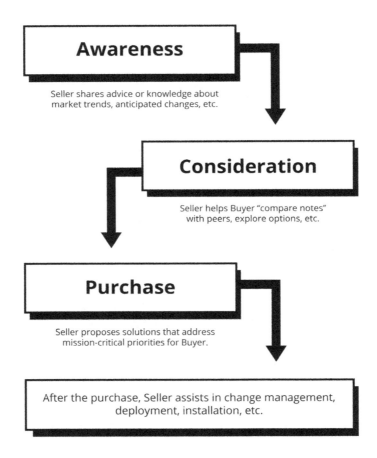

The building supply distribution company we described in the figure does a great job of offering extreme value to their customers. So does another customer of ours who provides shipping material to many of the large online retailers. They specially design their products to fit a variety of items to reduce shipping costs, while also maintaining a special recycling program for sustainability.

One of Michelle's favorite stories to tell is about another of our clients, a global metal recycling company. They are in an interesting business structured the opposite of traditional B2B sales teams. Their commercial (sales) team are the "buyers," purchasing scrap metal from manufacturing, demolition, scrap yards, municipalities, and other industrial uses. Their customers are the "sellers." In a highly competitive price-sensitive industry, one of their buyers has found a way to really stand out in her market. Prior to joining the metal recycling company, this buyer worked in banking and finance, and she ran a scrapyard for an investor. She leverages her business and entrepreneurial background as a differentiator; her customers call her for financial advice in addition to buying metal. This is the ultimate in strategic advisor positioning!

To be able to offer mission-critical insight, experiences, and advice to your prospects and customers, you must be diligent about all of the activities we group together as prospecting and pre-call planning.

- Really knowing your business and industry, inside and out.
- Learning as much as you can about your buyer—in some organizations, buyers.
- Understanding all the key players in decision-making, from the C-suite to the end user.
- Preparing carefully for every single interaction you have with your prospect or customer.

The best salespeople show their buyers that diligence and care is timeless.

Listening Is Still the Most Important Skill

The most successful salespeople are frequently the best at observing and adapting to people whom they are selling, which leads to better rapport and improves the conversations in a way that helps the customer get the best outcomes. Prospects only share what is important to them when this rapport leads to building trust; working together productively ultimately leads to greater trust. What trust means for a prospect or customer is believing that you and your organization and products or services are credible, you understand their needs, and you will deliver on every promise or commitment.

Study after study has shown (since the formal study of sales began early in the last century) that *listening* more than speaking may be the single most important skill that separates the top 10% of salespeople from the rest.

Recent research from Gong.io shows that sales professionals who are above 120% of quota talk less than they speak: Top reps talk 46% on sales calls and listen 54% of the time. In contrast, average reps talk 68% of the time and bottom reps talk 72% of the time.

That is a pretty big difference—more than 20%—between the top and the average!

According to the same research, women outperform men in both achieving quota and leading teams to quota—and it is the result of one key differentiator: listening. The study is pretty fascinating.[21] We just recently heard an anecdote that backs this up from one of the top sales professionals for the previously mentioned global metal recycling company. She attributes her success to differentiating herself from others—and listening. Her peers may go to an account, give them a price and move on—and miss out on valuable customer insight. This buyer acknowledged that she may not always get the job on which she originally bid, but she might uncover three more opportunities that she did not know about beforehand just by listening. The level of trust she has built with customers helps her win even when she is offering a lower price than her competitors for her customer's scrap metal.

Agility: Navigating Six Recent Transformative Changes in Sales

In much of the rest of this book, we are going to explore the concept of agility in a variety of ways. It is the factor that has separated those firms that experience longevity and profitability from those that just cannot keep going during times of stress. For now, let us just offer two examples to get the ball rolling:

A client of ours manufactures garage doors for commercial and residential applications. When COVID hit, their commercial business immediately dropped, but the residential side saw a large increase in demand. They accelerated a program to launch a website for all of their dealers, where residential users could browse designs and place orders without having to enter a showroom.

Another client created custom homes and could no longer meet face-to-face with their clients. They built a special delivery box filled with samples of materials and easy-to-follow instructions on how to join a virtual call to discuss the samples and finalize their home design.

At The Brooks Group, we believe that many of the changes on the global stage have sparked much-needed changes within specific companies and industries or hastened changes that were already underway. We have grouped our observations into six primary categories that we will present briefly here and explore in more detail in the chapters to come.

#1. The Biggest Change in the Modern History of Sales: Omnichannel Marketing and Sales

The last 20 years have seen an explosion in consumer transactions conducted over the Internet. It is not just that anyone, anywhere can purchase any item known to humankind 24/7 on Amazon. You can also find specifications, user manuals, warranty descriptions, live chat sessions, and more at the click of a touchpad or mouse or tap of a screen. You think about something you need, and a few keyboard clicks gets you the answer. What was Fred Flintstone's boss's name? Ask Siri. There is no need to wait for the nightly news or even SportsCenter on the hour—every story and score is a single search request away. If we want to know, we can find out (along with targeted ads and social media stories aimed our direction for days after we do that search, right?).

Except in much of the business world.

What is the status of my P.O.? How many units does my preferred supplier have in stock? Is it too late to get it on the truck for delivery in the morning? How do I order units after 6:00 p.m. or before 7:00 a.m.? For far too many businesses, these answers are still only accessed by a call, email, or text to a human at a supplier. That leads to customers too frequently receiving this ever-popular (but not very satisfying) response: "I'll have to look that up and get back to you."

During 2020, the digitalization of B2B sales accelerated rapidly. Your potential customers increasingly demanded self-service options for even complex B2B purchases. Many of the functions traditionally served by salespeople have been taken over by Internet-based tools and resources; buyers have grown in their ability to find information before ever engaging with a live human being.

> *Salespeople for a lighting component supplier we know were asked to put their products on the business site of a large online reseller, and they were concerned. They were afraid that selling via the online reseller would cannibalize their current brick-and-mortar distributors. What they found instead was a whole new world of contractors who worked during the day, then ordered supplies at night. After dinner they would log on and place their order for delivery the day after tomorrow, directly to the job site. That way, they could perform a full day of work and never have to make a supply run.*
>
> *That supplier discovered the power of omnichannel not just to sell more, but to reach an entire new market segment. It wasn't an either-or situation, but a both-and result!*

Examples like this begin to illustrate the importance—in fact, the necessity—of agility and openness to change for companies' continued success. What was your primary way of messaging customers when you started selling? Telephone, fax, email, voicemail, text, or social media? The last two have only become commonplace during the last ten years.

The influence of B2C marketing and sales strategies has made itself felt in all types of B2B marketplaces. It is changing how we think about roles and how they get filled, how we use technology and what technologies we choose, and ultimately, what our prospective customers experience as value in the buying process.

#2. The Buyer Is More Empowered Than Ever

In the pre-pandemic days before 2020, many sales professionals relied on being physically present or in person with customers as a new business creation sales strategy. In certain industries, they could wander into the client site and identify sales opportunities by inspecting equipment or talking to their key contacts. This is especially true of what we call "buddy sellers," or salespeople who rely on relationships—think drop-ins with doughnuts for the staff, business lunches, and golf outings—to develop accounts.

Many of the top decision makers today are Gen X, Millennials, and, now arriving on the scene, Gen Z. Data say they would rather complete sales transactions without ever speaking directly with a human. Customers have increasingly limited time for lunch, golf, or ballgames, but instead are replacing long, in-person meetings with calls (in some cases, video conferences). They want to be able to research vendors, products, and services online without the perceived pressure and time waste of a live sales interaction.

Not too long ago, one of our Boomer clients, who oversees the sales team for an industrial distribution company, told us, "Spreadsheets are ruining my business." That may sound strange, especially to those of us who love an Excel workbook for its power to organize and analyze data. What he meant, though, was that the next generation of new owners of companies are better educated than ever, seeking new ways to improve profitability and making fresh demands on suppliers. These buyers are using spreadsheets to track and compare potential supplier capabilities, sometimes ruling out (or in) a supplier before the supplier's sales organization ever has a chance to engage directly. Doughnuts and a baseball cap no longer win purchasing decisions.

Unfortunately, salespeople too often look like a deer in the headlights over these changes. They are being left behind by their own prospects and customers as a result. It is not just about the increased use of digital tools, though; it is about the effect that these tools have on the way buyers make purchase decisions and how value is delivered through sales professionals in this new way of buying.

#3. Sales Culture Takes Precedence

At The Brooks Group, we have been talking a lot in the last five years or so about sales culture and how important it is, especially in times of organizational stress. Because having a sales culture is basically a corporate soft skill, many leaders overlook it, thinking they cannot change it or that it is not even something they can measure. They will ask, "What does that really mean?" and, "Why can't I just drive my team based on metrics and numbers?"

Sure, there is an important place for metrics and numbers, and we will delve more into that in a later chapter. However, the human angle cannot be overlooked. In large part due to the pandemic, the idea of having a strong sales culture has jumped to the forefront—the more trust you have among folks in your sales organization, the more ability you have to work through change. This is true whether the changes have had to do with restructuring, compensation, territories, messages, methodologies, or whatever else. On teams where the culture was broken or there were difficulties, we have seen a lot of upheaval and much turnover. If you were only about trying to beat your number, month after month after month, suddenly when COVID hit, your team struggled.

In contrast, a good culture gets you through the worst of challenges.

People trust their managers and understand that hard decisions are made for the good of the business. They are willing to deliver extra because of the sense their company is as committed to them as they are to it. A 2018 University of Minnesota and MIT research project saw new bosses who like to collaborate share credit for transactions with their team, in general produced an average 30% increase in sales. On the other hand, new bosses who set unrealistic expectations and ended up micromanaging saw a 7.5% decrease in sales.[22]

Our prediction is that those cultures that are struggling will continue to see far more turnover than those who have stronger sales cultures. If you are aware of the importance of a strong sales culture, you are probably doing a better job than most already at ensuring your organization has one. Virtually every company can do better or do more, though.

#4. No More Lone Wolf Selling: Team Selling Gets the Wins

The salesperson as a lone wolf is an endangered species, nearly extinct in most industries. B2B purchases are business to business, not single person to business. A boss of Russ's used to say, "Sales sells the first unit; the rest of the company sells the second." The point was everyone had to do their job for the customer to be satisfied and continue to buy. In today's selling environment, buyers and end-users expect even more than that. They want to have a 100% seamless experience with your organization, wherein every person they choose to contact is informed, responsive to the client's requests, and able to take action.

We have multiple clients who are working to cross-train their service or implementation team—think service or repair techs, engineers, consultants, and so on—to ask a few more questions in order to spot potential needs for additional projects. They do not try to turn them into full-time salespeople, but they are training them to spot areas where their clients have issues and where the consulting company has expertise. Other clients of ours are re-working their compensation plans to reward people for collaborative selling approaches. This goes beyond traditional "team selling"

> *The more trust you have among folks in your sales organization, the more ability you have to work through change.*

techniques to a new approach, where the selling organization is unified from the buyer's perspective and professionals across the organization all "own the customer." It requires empowering many sales or sales-adjacent roles with the authority and ability to solve the customer's problem no matter what. That sometimes can be as simple as answering a question or as complex as changing key order attributes.

This is a lesson medical device and supplies companies learned after the passage of the Affordable Care Act in 2009. No longer could a surgeon or clinical lead take a liking to a product and require its purchase for use in their department going forward. Now there is a structure of supply chain executives, value committees, and buying structures that must be navigated to win. Most firms have moved to a team selling approach with different people responsible for the departments and surgery centers, the carpeted portions of a hospital (for supply chain and executives), and for buying groups.

#5. Everyone Seems to Have Metric Mania

And it is a mania with many symptoms. Nearly every one of our clients asks us about metrics. Do they have the right metrics, or Key Performance Indicators (KPIs)? What is the right number of KPIs? How often should they review/change them? Am I getting the right results from the KPIs I measure?

During COVID, companies did not know whether to (or how to) adjust their KPIs. What was the right number of calls per week when they were virtual instead of in-person? Would they be changing KPIs for virtual selling only to change them back when the pandemic was over? Many of them did nothing—possibly because they did not know what to do.

Sales leaders know there are always two critical metrics: revenue and margin. But those can only be measured after the end of the financial period. So, the industry has exploded with numbers of calls, presentations, measurements of average P.O. size, add-ons, shipments of new products, new logos or customers, revived customers, etc., that can, in some cases, indicate the trajectory of the sales team's performance.

Measurement will always be a part of a sales team. In many ways, behind manufacturing, sales is the second-most measured department. But too many or the wrong metrics can not only hold a team back, but they also can drive counterproductive behaviors. When they first seek our advice, most of our Software-as-a-Service (SaaS) clients are measuring demonstrations performed, causing many salespeople to rush to the demo without understanding even what should be demonstrated! The result is lots of demos, a nearly equal number of confused or unconvinced prospects, and a funnel that sees far too many deals fade away.

Successful sales teams understand the real levers for driving business and watch a small but powerful set of metrics to achieve consistent performance. This is an excellent application of Occam's Razor—the simplest solution is almost always the best.

#6. Aggressive Cost Competition Is the Norm

For many years, Proctor & Gamble rotated purchasing people every six months so they would not develop "too-friendly" relationships with their suppliers' salespeople. The idea behind these term limits was the perception that when purchasers built relationships with specific salespeople, they would favor these companies over lower-priced suppliers when making purchasing decisions. (Of course, this totally ignores the tremendous value of deeply understanding requirements and products and demonstrates a lack of trust between management and its purchasing employees.)

Now, other companies are using this blunt force method, rotating purchasers and causing too many salespeople to focus on selling price above every other element of a sale. In doing so, they are often performing "penny wise and pound foolish."

Is this increased pressure from purchasing departments a "good" change or a "bad" change for salespeople? Well, it is bad for salespeople who do not understand the value their product or service brings to their customers—the salespeople who fail to understand the customer's business beyond purchasing, and who think being friendly with their buyers is enough for success. But for those quality salespeople who can grasp the larger picture of a customer's business, it is a non-issue.

A client of ours sold industrial ball bearings that were significantly more expensive on a per-unit basis than competitors' products. Purchasing kept asking for a price, and our client kept losing the business—until they spoke to plant managers and discovered that production lines had to be shut down for 24 hours every quarter to replace all the bearings. Our client realized that its bearings offered much longer life, saving two line shutdowns a year (twice instead of four times a year). The result was the manufacturer ended up paying more per bearing but saving hundreds of thousands of dollars a year in reduced plant shut down time and increased production.

Another client struggled to introduce a new line of personal protective equipment (PPE) into select markets due to a higher pricing structure. Again, purchasing said, "no." But by working directly with the users and performing fit and comfort testing, our client became the preferred brand. The cost of a unit of PPE compared to happy staff (not to mention better retention) was insignificant.

The Successful Hybrid Seller Guides the Buyer's Journey

Sales professionals who are most successful and least stressed out are those who have learned how to sell in this environment: hybrid sellers. These salespeople recognize how critical it is to join their prospects' and customers' buying journey on their timeframes, and they understand how to use a combination of virtual and in-person selling tools to get results for their customers and themselves. We believe that it is this realization that needed to happen for sales professionals; a global pandemic just exacerbated and accelerated the change in attitude and approach.

Hybrid seller: A salesperson who recognizes how critical it is to join buyers on their timeframes, and understands how to use a combination of virtual and in-person selling tools to get results for their customers and themselves.

When salespeople enter later in the buying process, they must understand that customers are more knowledgeable, perhaps even overloaded with knowledge. Today's seller's goal should be to help prospects and customers focus on the important considerations, not be what we jokingly call a "talking webpage." A consistent playbook/process that is designed to help your salespeople stay in step with your prospects/customers as they navigate their way to a purchase decision is an essential tool in your sales team's toolkit. (Shameless self-promotion: The Brooks Group's IMPACT Selling System is one such process.)

Salespeople must be more intentional with their sales approach, setting appointments, crafting sales objectives, sending agendas, and engaging in more robust business conversations. As one sales manager told us recently, "When my salespeople are able to make contact with their clients, they better have something more meaningful to say than, 'How's business?'"

Consistent and rapid change—plus heavy competition for market share—means there is a lot of conflicting information out there in every possible medium, from print ads with QR codes to blog and social media

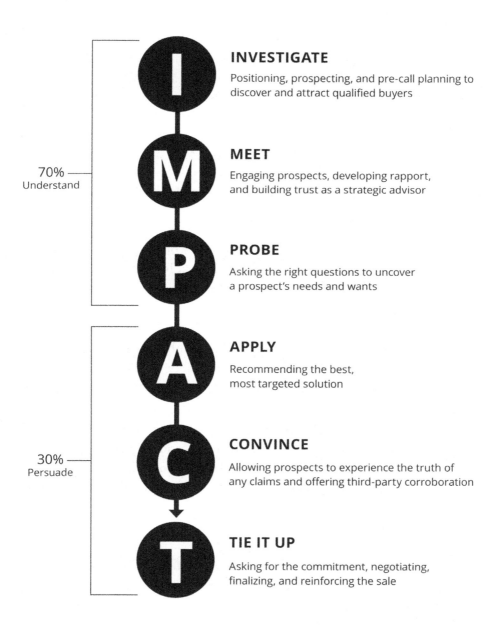

70%
Understand

30%
Persuade

INVESTIGATE
Positioning, prospecting, and pre-call planning to discover and attract qualified buyers

MEET
Engaging prospects, developing rapport, and building trust as a strategic advisor

PROBE
Asking the right questions to uncover a prospect's needs and wants

APPLY
Recommending the best, most targeted solution

CONVINCE
Allowing prospects to experience the truth of any claims and offering third-party corroboration

TIE IT UP
Asking for the commitment, negotiating, finalizing, and reinforcing the sale

posts. Everyone is out there trying their hardest to move qualified prospects to that elusive sales meeting (whether in-person or virtual). Every day, buyers are bombarded—according to *Texas CEO Magazine* in 2021, more than 7.5 million blog posts, 2 million LinkedIn posts, and 100 million Instagram ads are sent flying through cyberspace in a single 24-hour period.[23] And that's a problem: Exactly half of decision-makers say the information tends to be overwhelming. All that information overload could cause your buyer to tune out—but not if you do it right.

It is helpful to look at an analysis of the three types of thought leaders in sales, based on research from Gartner:

- **The More-Is-Better Approach:** These are the salespeople who simply cannot stop talking! They dominate every conversation and drop off a two-inch binder filled with information and catalogs on the product—or append 15 attachments to an email. Are you surprised that clients become overwhelmed and either do not look at it at all or flip through it very quickly without any real comprehension?

- **The Storyteller:** Though there is great value in storytelling, if you make it just about your experiences, the client will become concerned that you have not done adequate research about how other buyers deal with the same information, or do not have a broad enough set of experiences to draw upon in providing support to them.

- **The Hybrid Seller:** Positioned as a sales guide, the hybrid seller learns where the top portion of the thought leadership curve is (the point at which the buyer becomes overwhelmed) and stays in the zone of understanding and trust. A good hybrid seller knows the right questions to ask, uses the proper tools, and makes sure that the client is making a rational, educated decision versus going "on their gut." This is a key skill of hybrid sellers.

The hybrid seller knows how to adapt to the audience/buyer; for a CxO, that means communicating how a product or service complements the company's strategic objectives, minimizes risk, contributes to innovation, etc. We will talk more about this in the coming chapters. Regardless of whom your point of contact is, the important skill is the ability to distill the volume of available information down to the most relevant points for the buyer, and then relay those points in a concise, uncomplicated way.

So clearly, a hybrid seller can seem like an oasis in the desert—someone who brings order out of chaos in these days of information overload. Best suited to help reduce skepticism and increase loyalty, this type of sales guide is a trusted resource for his or her customers. In the rest of this book, we will talk a lot more about how hybrid sellers ensure their prospects and customers have the kind of buying experiences they want and expect.

Key Takeaways from This Chapter

- In the absence of a value interpreter, every product or service essentially becomes the same. When buyers are involving salespeople later and later in the buying process—if at all—it is imperative that your sales team are effective hybrid sellers.
- Quality = Performance = Value for the Cost
- The most agile companies have navigated six recent transformative changes in sales:

1. **Omnichannel marketing and sales has been the biggest change in the modern history of sales.** The influence of B2C marketing and sales strategies on B2B marketplaces is changing how we think about roles and how they get filled, how we use technology and what technologies we choose, and ultimately, what our prospective customers experience as value in the buying process.

2. **The buyer is more empowered than ever.** Buyers have access at their fingertips to track and compare potential supplier capabilities, sometimes ruling out (or in) a supplier before the supplier's sales organization ever has a chance to engage directly.

3. **Your organization's sales culture takes precedence.** The more trust you have among folks in your sales organization, the more ability you have to work through change.

4. **No more lone wolf selling: Team selling gets the wins.** Buyers want a 100% seamless experience with your organization, wherein every person they choose to contact is informed, responsive to the client's requests, and able to take action.

5. **Everyone seems to have metric mania.** The most successful sales teams understand the real levers for driving business and watch a small but powerful set of metrics to achieve consistent performance.

6. **Aggressive cost competition is the norm.** If you are able to reduce risk and/or help a customer innovate, you have built unique value for your business and for your customer. And that will ensure your salespeople can focus their customers on the value your solutions bring, not the dollar amount they cost.

- Hybrid sellers are salespeople who recognize how critical it is to join their prospects' and customers' buying journey on their timeframes.

Ask Yourself

- How are we reducing risk and/or helping our customers innovate?
- Where are our buyers looking for information about possible solutions to common problems in our industry?
- Have I established a reasonable set of metrics to track the most important performance factors that are relevant right now for my team?
- How can we improve the experience our customers have with my organization? Where are the hiccups and stumbles that need to be addressed?

 CHAPTER 2 FREE TOOL
Agility Audit

https://brooksgroup.com/download-tools/

Chapter

3

Buyers Are More Empowered Than Ever

The agility and resiliency required of professional B2B sales teams in response to the tremendous speed of change that we have described are here to stay. Organizationally and individually, your sales team must be ready and able to make frequent, effective pivots in how you prospect, approach, and sell to new and existing customers.

The best way your sales team can prepare for the shifts that will naturally be required for profitability in the coming years is to pay attention to how buyers look for information and manage the buying process and decisions within it. Changes in technology, the economy, market segment trends, and other factors only matter so much. If you are following the *buyer*[24], you will have the best chance of getting a deal signed—regardless of other situational, temporary factors. Because you will be focused on understanding your customer's organizational buying process, you will simplify the buying experience for them. And you will be rewarded with better engagement and faster sales cycles. If you guide buyers—whether they are CxOs or procurement professionals, prospects or existing customers—on their buying journey, along the way they will learn to trust your knowledge, observations, and advice.

Focus on Customer Wants and Needs for Leverage

If we consider a universe of salespeople, they typically will fall along a normal distribution that looks something like this:

- 20% sell enough to barely get by (or less)

- 60% are average or slightly above/below average
- 20% are top performers who deliver 75%–80% of sales

What is very interesting is that there is a marked difference between where the top 20% are focused, as opposed to the bottom 20%. Sales success is driven fundamentally not by skills, attitudes, product knowledge, or luck (though of course those do come into play). Instead, it is driven by where the salesperson's primary focus is most of the time.

As you can see, the bottom 20% are focused primarily on survival and quota. Especially in times of stress, most sellers tend to gravitate toward survival mode. Unfortunately, buyers know it and will use it to their advantage. We have had sellers in our client organizations tell us that they know their customers will wait until the end of the month to buy because they know the sellers will discount in order to close deals when they are desperate to meet quota.

The middle 60% focus on product/service, personal income, and/or ego. We often refer to this segment by its initials, P.I.E. It comes from being fed nothing but product information in company training sessions, so salespeople subconsciously think "if that is what I'm taught, the customers must care," so they show up and talk product, feature, product, feature, ad nauseam.

The top 20% focus on buyer needs and wants. Further, within the top 20%, there is a distinction: The top 10% focus on what their prospects really want. They are all about satisfying buyers in the way the buyers want to be satisfied. They understand that every buyer has a unique combination of attributes driving their organization to select a product or service. These sellers want to be sure they understand those attributes, and they position their offering to satisfy—even delight—the customer. They also increasingly focus on the way in which a buyer buys—the buyer's process—to be sure to stay in step with the buyer.

How does your sales team address buyer process changes? Have they stopped making assumptions about what buyers want? We strongly encourage you to get more information about how decisions for your type of products or services are made so your sales team can make progress with the buyer—on their timeframe and with their priorities and strategies in mind. Because change happens so quickly, sales professionals must continuously seek an understanding of what buyers expect from the sales process.

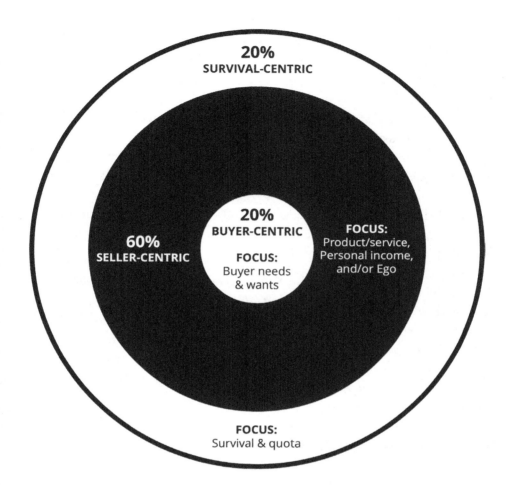

Increasingly here at The Brooks Group, our sellers have seen functional buyers in Sales or Learning & Development unsure of how their companies buy. The maze of Legal, Purchasing, and C-suite signoffs is confusing to navigate, and they continually ask us to help them move an agreement through this system.

The New Approach to Professional Selling Is Buyer-Informed

Since at least the 1980s, sales professionals likely have been trained (either formally or through experience) in various approaches to selling that are focused on selling value. Whether known as solution selling, insight selling, partnership selling, consultative selling, or some other name, the basic premise is that the salesperson consults with the buyer to uncover and diagnose pain points in their business and then recommends solutions that will alleviate that pain. The idea is that if you have built trust with your prospects and customers, you can engage them in productive conversations around their needs (and wants, of course). When you present your solution to the prospect, you then can connect the value of what you sell within the context of their business problem.

Selling value was certainly a 100% better approach than old-school, high-pressure sales techniques. Over the last 30 years or so, B2B salespeople have become successful by serving as valued business resources for their customers. However, well before the COVID-19 pandemic hit, changes were in the air. Selling value is only part of the picture; the other

> *Sales success is driven fundamentally not by skills, attitudes, product knowledge, or luck (though of course those do come into play). Instead, it is driven by where the salesperson's primary focus is most of the time.*

key is learning *how* buyers prepare themselves and their companies to make purchase decisions. Today, getting results as a B2B salesperson is achieved by buyer-centered selling, seeing through the buyer's eyes and on the buyer's timeline.

In order to make profitable sales, professional sellers must take into account and be attuned to the journey buyers make in exploring solutions and arriving at a final purchase decision: Think of it as a quest that each buyer is on, searching for the right path forward. You can do everything in your power as a professional salesperson to follow your own sales process, but you cannot force a buyer to move more quickly along in their journey than they are ready to move. Being in tune with your prospects and customers lets you anticipate and respond to changes rapidly and effectively.

The Evolution of Corporate Decision Making

Increasingly at The Brooks Group, our clients are seeking more than training. Though that has been our core competency for over 40 years, recently we have realized that inside of our training is a key understanding of how great sales organizations operate. Our conversations with prospects typically start on a training need and evolve into a broader discussion of how their sales organization approaches the market, measures its success through key performance indicators (KPIs), or even how they can take concepts learned in training and fully integrate them into their sales operations.

Let's take a quick look at an example of one of our other clients—a packaging materials company—who is getting it right.

> *One of our client's existing customers stated they were going to put their contract out to bid, "just to be sure we're getting the best price." Instead of panicking, the sales team went to work, looking through the customer's annual report and strategy goal-by-goal, connecting how they helped the customer achieve each strategic initiative described in the annual report.*
>
> *Within a few days, the salesperson presented the results to the customer. Guess what? The project never went to bid. Our client did have to make a price concession, but not only was it far less than it would have been if they had to fight against lower priced competitors in a bid process, they also got a commitment for larger purchase volumes going forward.*

There are a couple of things that went right in this case. First off, our client's salesperson was clearly respected by the buyer—the fact that the buyer gave the salesperson a heads-up about the potential bid situation was one indicator, and the other was that he took the salesperson's call a few days later! Second, investing in our client's materials and solutions actually *did* have a measurable ROI for their customer—they had definitive proof that what they claimed was accurate.

This example also brings up an important point for us:

Selling to existing customers versus new prospects is different in a key aspect. When selling to a new customer, sales must create a discomfort with the status quo—so that working with a new vendor will be perceived as the right choice to improve the situation. Yet when selling to an existing customer, sales must make sure the customer is comfortable with the status quo. Many sales organizations miss this difference.

We see sellers either underestimate the impact or fear of change on new prospects (especially with multiple decision makers) and then take comfort with the status quo for granted with existing accounts. In the current environment, even existing customers are scrutinizing their vendor relationships to maximize value, so sales professionals must be sure they do not fail to continue reinforcing and demonstrating the value they bring to the ongoing relationship.

Buyers Have a Difficult Job (No, Really, They Do)

As sales professionals ourselves, we know that many days it feels like sales must be the hardest job out there. That has been especially true in the last few years, when so much has seemed to change so rapidly about how our prospects and clients research and make purchase decisions. Now, not only have C-suite folks gotten more deeply invested in purchase decisions, but, even pre-pandemic, more and more organizations already had shifted to procurement departments as a central orchestrator of the purchasing process. This happened not simply to cut costs and source supplies, but to streamline operations and even uncover new sources of revenue.

In our own work at The Brooks Group, we are seeing more decisions move from the VP of Sales to a combination of Learning & Development and Sales, or (more recently) global task forces responsible for training. This reflects another major trend in B2B buying: cross-functional team decision making. In these cases, there is a representative from every affected business unit involved in reviewing and assessing potential solutions and solution providers.

This is shown very clearly in our work with medical device clients. In the past, new products were evaluated by surgeons, who had the exclusive power to change hospital or surgery center preference: "Win the doc, win the deal." Those days are no more because now every medical center has established a cross-disciplinary value committee to review changes in the purchase of any device or supply.

These medical institutions are looking at patient, operational, and financial outcomes to drive a decision to change devices. As it was explained to us by a hospital COO, if a device can demonstrate superior patient outcomes, it is approved easily. But if the outcomes are not clear, or even minimal, and if (as is usually the case) the device costs more than the old one, organizations say, "No, thank you," to the salesperson AND the surgeon.

As buyers do so much more research before ever engaging with a seller, a lot of salespeople grow increasingly frustrated. We hear frequent griping that "I can't get a meeting," "They aren't willing to review my new product," "Can't they see this new offering is so much better?" or even, "I'm seeing a lot more RFQ/RFPs without knowing they are coming." If you've been known to say any of these things, you're not wrong: It can be frustrating.

However, the salespeople we've seen consistently meet or exceed quota are those who realize that buyers have very frustrating and challenging jobs, too.

How do you feel about that statement? Would you agree, or do you need some convincing? Hear us out.

In the 2021 State of Buyer and Seller Alignment report,[25] Sales Mastery noted:

"From past studies we have noted that where there has been a shock to the economy and/or business climate there can be a shift in the number of stakeholders who are involved in approving large purchases. Across study participants we saw an average of 6.2 decision makers taking part in current buy cycles. When asked how this compared to pre-COVID, 20% shared that the number of people involved had increased, where 57% reported the number remained the same, and 23% stated the number of decision makers was lower."

Add to that the absolutely overwhelming access to data about possible solutions, comparisons of potential vendors, and constantly evolving technologies out there, and is it any surprise that we have seen estimates that nearly 50% of companies stop the research and exploration process without ever buying anything? Frequently, buyers face decision fatigue and just cannot build consensus among their own team about priorities and the right direction to take.

Today's buyers really do have a hard job.

Salespeople can unintentionally (or maybe intentionally?) make it even worse. Some overuse the "we want to partner with you" phrase without supporting it with real value. They often trumpet the phrase but never ask the essential underlying questions: What can I help my prospect or customer accomplish? What do they need to have a comfortable buying process? If you can uncover this information and get to that point, you can *be* a partner in fact—not just a supplier.

> *A few years ago, we worked with an ocean freight company who worked with large retailers to import goods from all over the world. In conversations with these customers, our client discovered they needed greater predictability of arrival of merchandise—a delay of even a few days could cause outages that affected sales and customer satisfaction. Our client was already providing details on ship departure and arrival dates, but their customers needed more.*
> *Partnering together, our client created a new class of service that could ensure priority customer's containers were offloaded as a part of the first 10% of containers delivered. That reduced the delivery time window to within 48 hours of the ship's arrival at the port.*
> *A true problem was solved, retailers had assurances of product delivery and the new service was offered at a slight premium that made it a more profitable offering for our client. All parties benefited—the definition of a true partnership.*

"How's Business?" Just Will Not Cut It

We can almost hear you thinking an important question: "You told me that buyers are doing a huge amount of research before ever allowing sales to the table. Now, you have just told me I have to be a partner for my buyers throughout the selling process. What gives? How can I do that if they will not talk to me until they have done a ton of research on their own?"

At The Brooks Group, ever since our founder Bill Brooks launched the IMPACT Selling System in the 1980s, we have placed a lot of emphasis on all the things that need to happen before a salesperson can present a recommendation to their prospect or customer. The first few steps of IMPACT Selling are all about effectively prospecting so you are only making sales calls on truly qualified prospects, positioning yourself and your organization, and getting ready for each unique sales meeting. They are also about meeting your prospects and customers in a way that builds rapport and trust so that you can begin engaging on the real issues that affect their business. In our minds, those things are pretty logical and timeless, regardless of what steps your buyer is taking in order to make a purchase decision.

In the "olden days" of just 15 years or so ago, we all knew pharmaceutical salespeople who were trained to drop by physicians' offices with lunch and product samples in hand. One medical office manager we know quipped that she never had to bring lunch to work, as a different salesperson brought lunch for everyone every day! The idea was that by being on-site and getting "face time" with their doctors, the pharma reps would be top of mind when the physicians were recommending medications to their patients. At the same time, the reps would be learning the treatment practices and typical patients for the practice.

While the friendly sales rep "just stopping by" approach was decreasing already, the COVID era brought it to a full stop. Somehow, hybrid sellers find ways to build rapport and trust—and be top of mind—for their prospects and customers without frequently being on-site, in person.

According to Forrester, buyers average 27 meaningful interactions with a selling organization. Most of those interactions are now self-guided (54%) versus personal engagement (46%).[26]

Somehow, sales professionals must prove that they are what Gartner refers to as "sense-making salespeople," who are trusted resources able to play pivotal roles in guiding buyers toward reasonable solutions.

And this is not limited to pharma. If 77% of B2B buyers do not talk to a salesperson until they have done their own research[27] and office- or plant-floor drop-ins are not as productive, sales *must* find a way to be involved earlier in the buying process. This requires that they make shifts in how they approach the sales process, adjusting it to complement the buying process, on the buyer's timeline. They need to change their expectations of what meetings and interactions need to happen, when, and how they happen. (It appears that the model of selling going forward does not have an in-person meeting until the buyer is ready to have a deeper, more informed discussion—perhaps even *after* the contract is signed.)

Remember the sales manager who told us his sales reps need to have something more meaningful than, "How's business?" to say when they are making contact with their clients and prospective clients? That is such a great observation, and we believe it goes well beyond that. Sales organizations as a whole need to acknowledge that buyer preferences have changed and

> *Somehow, hybrid sellers find ways to build rapport and trust—and be top of mind—for their prospects and customers without frequently being on-site, in person.*

vary from individual to individual and firm to firm. We need to ensure that we are providing what the buyer needs and wants through every channel and stage of the buying process. This requires alignment across sales and marketing functions too.

Is the content that your marketing department is providing for buyer education clear? Does it differentiate and contribute to the trust-building process? (We will definitely talk more about the marketing and sales alignment piece later in this book.) The only way it will be is if, when, and how your salespeople interact with buyers is based on what the buyer wants—not what you prefer.

Selling System vs. Buyer's Journey

We mentioned it earlier, and many of our readers know that we teach a selling system called IMPACT Selling. It is a proven approach to positioning, prospecting, pre-call planning, building rapport and trust, asking the right questions of the right people at the right time, applying targeted solutions, closing deals, and gaining commitments so you have the best chance of happy —and repeat—customers. If practiced right, a selling system like IMPACT will follow neatly along a map of the buyer's journey.

We talked in Chapter 2 about the Awareness-Consideration-Decision model of the buyer's journey. It is a great starting point and, back in 2019, Inflexion Point, a company focused on B2B selling, posted a blog that delineated the steps of the buyer's journey further.[28] We like it because it really clarifies with more specificity what is going on behind the scenes of the buyer's decision-making process:

1. **Unconcerned:** Even if they have a problem, they are either unaware of it or not worried about it right now.
2. **Disturbed:** Something has drawn the buyer's attention to a problem or opportunity, and they are feeling some sense of urgency about assessing it.
3. **Investigating:** They've identified the challenge and have begun researching trusted sources of information and building a list of potential solutions.
4. **Defining:** The buyer understands clearly what their challenge is and believes there are solutions available. Now, they are making their short list of solution providers based on a defined decision criterion: Will the solution address their challenge?
5. **Selecting:** The buyer's decision-making team works together to identify their preferred solution and supplier/partner. (Interestingly, Inflexion Point notes that, "...If stakeholders fail to achieve consensus [it's] likely to be a decision to 'do nothing.'")
6. **Verifying:** This is where the buyer is looking for confirmation and affirmation that they made the right choice in moving forward with their chosen solution and negotiated terms that will benefit them.
7. **Confirming:** The rubber hits the road here, as this is the contract signing go-ahead from the client's top management, legal team, and so on.

Throughout the seven steps described above, there are critical interconnected processes of consensus-building and validation that must happen consistently and coherently across the buyer's decision-making organization.

What we like so much about this more complex view of the buyer's journey is that it provides a clear roadmap for where hybrid sellers should engage and add value. It also draws attention to the fact that the buying process most often involves a team of stakeholders. These are key points to which professional salespeople pay attention.

The Seller's Process *Must* Map to the Buyer's Journey

We will look at each stage and show how our IMPACT Selling system maps onto it next.

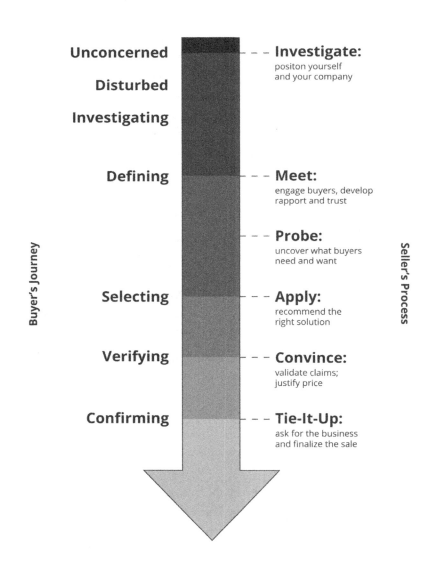

So where are the opportunities for sales? They are throughout the buyer's journey, actually. There is a lot of great data to support this in a 2021 survey report released by Sales Mastery.[29]

Ideally, the objective for sales is to be properly positioned and get involved in the client's buying process, preferably ahead of the investigating phase, at least, when buyers are starting to identify possible solutions to evaluate. This is occurring in only 43% of the cases reported by study participants. Of note, this is a noticeable decrease from the findings in the 2018 study, where that percentage was 56% (30% for clarifying needs and 26% for identifying solutions).

At the other end of the buying process, other signs of concern emerge for sales organizations. One in five study participants had completed the defining and selection phases on their own. It is only when they want to verify and negotiate or, more concerning, have purchased and are ready to implement the solution, that they finally decided to engage with salespeople. This is double the 2018 figure: only 10% of buying firms waiting that long in the process to connect with sellers.

For many companies, the buy cycle has become longer. The 2021 survey found that 60% of participants reported that additional scrutiny was being given to purchasing budgeted items during COVID. Further, having established relationships is a key advantage for salespeople. To help quantify this advantage, 65% of existing vendors were able to complete the buy cycle in three months or less. This percentage fell to 36% when buyers were dealing with a new vendor. This is important information:

- If you are trying to convince a prospect to drop an existing vendor in favor of your new solution, you will have to make a *very* compelling case for making change.
- In contrast, if *you* are the existing vendor and wanting to keep your account or increase client spend, you will need to emphasize comfort with the status quo.

REMINDER: This is a great place to consider the Value Formula for a new prospect and for an existing client. How are they similar? How is the value you bring in each case different?

According to our research at The Brooks Group in October 2021, 57% of sales leaders surveyed indicated that their sales cycle had gotten longer, and 33% of that group indicated their sales cycle was significantly longer. (That is only a slight improvement over 2020, when 61% of sales leaders noted that their sales cycle had increased since the COVID-19 pandemic began.)

Also in our October 2021 survey:

- 68% of sales leaders indicated that buyer engagement through digital channels had increased
- 58% responded that the number of calls required to close the sale had increased
- 64% noted an increase in changes in buyer priorities or purchase requirements during the sales process

This last point seems particularly crucial. If a seller does not get aligned—and *stay* aligned—with the buyer's journey, they may miss these changes and end up presenting a solution that misses the target. Worse yet, they may miss the opportunity to help shape new priorities or requirements, losing the chance to serve as a true sales guide.

If you do not have the right salespeople on your team, they are unlikely to be willing and/or able to serve as sales guides for the prospects and customers that make your company profitable. In the next chapter, we are going to delve into what your organization's sales culture has to do with the success of your salespeople's efforts and show you how to choose salespeople whose values and motivations align with those of your company.

Key Takeaways from This Chapter

- Professional salespeople can do everything in their power to follow their sales process, but it is impossible to force a buyer to move more quickly along in their journey than they are ready to move. In order to make profitable sales, professional sellers must take into account and be attuned to the journey buyers make in exploring solutions and arriving at a final purchase decision.
- The salespeople who most consistently meet or exceed quota are those who realize that buyers have very frustrating and challenging jobs too.

- Opportunities for selling lie at points everywhere along the buyer's journey.

- The top 20% of sales professionals focus on what their prospects really want and need. They are all about satisfying buyers in the way the buyers want to be satisfied. They understand that every buyer has a unique combination of attributes driving their organization to select a product or service.

- Ensuring that your company is providing what the buyer needs and wants through every channel and stage of the buying process requires alignment across corporate functions, especially and most importantly sales and marketing.

Ask Yourself

- Am I exploring with my salespeople how their buyers are navigating the decision-making journey—in cases when they choose our solutions *and* cases when they are not?

- Are my salespeople engaging at the most effective points in the buyer's journey? If not, how can I coach them to make adjustments?

- What factors make it most compelling for an existing customer to continue doing business with my company? What factors make it most compelling for a prospect to switch to my company's products or services?

- Which of my salespeople, when invited into a buyer's process, can bring significant value? How are they demonstrating it to the prospect in that first meeting?

CHAPTER 3 FREE TOOL
The IMPACT Selling Process Guide

https://brooksgroup.com/download-tools/

Chapter

4

Culture First, Compensation Second

Sixty-nine percent of workers say the coronavirus pandemic is the most stressful time of their professional career—more than 9/11 and the 2008 Great Recession.[30] One in four workers plan to look for new opportunities with a new employer once the pandemic has subsided.[31] As we write this in late 2021, we are seeing evidence of "The Great Resignation" every week in the news. The number of workers who quit their jobs in April 2021 broke the previous all-time U.S. record; then, in July and August, that number increased again.[32]

Linda Pophal, a marketing and communications strategist, has observed six reasons why people quit their jobs as the pandemic dragged on.[33] We believe that every one of these six potential reasons has something to do with their company's culture:

1. They have gotten a taste for work-hour flexibility.
2. They are burned out.
3. They are not feeling connected to the company culture.
4. They want to continue to work remotely.
5. They do not see a clear path forward.
6. They want to spend their time focused on doing meaningful work.

Did you notice that none of the six has anything to do with how much they are paid? Sure, our own research has historically shown time and time again that top salespeople are frequently motivated first by financial gain. But that has rarely been the only motivator, and, by all indicators as Millennials and Gen Z salespeople continue to make their presence known in the workplace, it may recede even further in importance.

> *One of our clients designed its compensation plan for inside salespeople so that once they have achieved their daily targets—calls, meetings booked, etc.—they are able to end their workday. Where Boomers would have stuck around for more financial incentives, this team of younger sellers valued time off more. As early as 2015, Glassdoor reported that 79% of employees "would prefer new or additional benefits to a pay increase." Those benefits include better insurance, performance bonuses, flexible schedules, tuition reimbursement, wellness programs, and more.[34]*

We will talk more about this in a later chapter, but there have been significant changes in how the most successful, profitable sales organizations are structuring themselves—largely in response to the digitalization of purchase decisions. These sales teams are placing far greater emphasis on collaboration, team-based selling, and the value they bring to their customers than sales teams of old ever did. All of these new developments are necessitating a new approach to company culture—and new attention being paid to the values behind that culture.

A Sales-Focused Company Is a Customer-Focused Company

It goes without saying (but we are going to say it anyway) that sales should be the first priority of your sales organization. But in order to make those sales, great sales leaders engage the entire company to establish a sales-focused culture across all functional units and departments. In a sales culture, making sales is not just a goal, it is a way of life—and, more importantly, it is a way of life that everyone in the company is a part of and everyone works toward. All the different departments understand that they are part of a larger whole, and the entire company works toward improving sales in whatever ways are appropriate for their roles.

While "sales" is a general goal focus for all employees, more specifically, they should be focused on the customer: who they are, what they want, and how to keep them happy. We hope this is already at the forefront of your salespeople's minds, but it is not as easy for someone in, say, IT, to think about how the customers are affected by what they do. It is essential that your organizational culture is always, always tuned into your customers' needs, wants, and ultimate welfare—the lifeblood of your company.

We know that as a sales leader, it is a reality that you may or may not be able to make transformative cultural change across your organization. A lot depends on your role, the size of your company, its culture right now, and your own personality and temperament. We assume, though, that if you are in a position of leadership in a sales organization, you can make an impact on the culture of your sales team.

What If Your Company Does Not Have a Customer-Oriented Culture?

So, what do you do as a sales leader if your company does not embrace a customer-oriented culture? Start selling. In our work with clients, we see many sales leaders who are frustrated that other departments are not as customer-centric as sales would like. Our encouragement to them every time—recognize that other organizations have charters and goals like your customers do—they are not always focused on what you think would be best. So, build relationships, bring information, introduce them to key customers, and thank them when they help. Create a vision of how their charter and being more customer-focused are actually in alignment. And when you "close the sale," all will benefit, inside and outside your organization.

That is what this chapter is about: Ensuring that your sales team has a culture not just of making sales via a buyer-centered process, but adaptability to change that affects their jobs, their customers, and your company as a whole.

For some of you, a discussion about culture seems too soft and mushy. Yet sales culture is undisputedly more than feelings. It is the aggregate expectations of individuals about how they will treat customers and how they will be treated as employees. Peter Drucker is famous for recognizing "culture eats strategy for lunch" because unspoken expectations of behavior shout more loudly than anything.

We all admire the NYFD for racing up the stairs of the World Trade Center on September 11. But what made them do that? Culture. If ever given the chance to stay at a Ritz Carlton, we love the service driven by their culture. Take a moment and think about your sales team. What is your culture really encouraging? What is it letting slip? And, most important, how does it need to change for today's selling environment?

Strategy + Culture = A Winning Combination

Organizations have two "levers" that empower and manage overall effectiveness—strategy and culture.[35] Strategy provides the explicit goals and clarity/focus for decision making. Strategy is concrete, and it relies on formal plans. An organization's revenue goals, for instance, are measurable. We can orient a team around them.

On the other hand, culture is the implicit social order of an organization. It expresses goals through the company's values and beliefs, and guides activity through shared norms. Culture defines:

- what is encouraged, discouraged, shared, accepted, or rejected
- how strategy is executed

With the early 2020s straining so many organizations' strategies, culture has rapidly begun taking center stage. A year-and-a-half into the COVID pandemic, more employees than ever evaluated how their employers had managed the pandemic, both from a business perspective and a cultural perspective. Time and time again, we have seen that organizations that aligned strategy and culture have generated more revenue, likely because they retain more good employees, have greater employee *and* customer satisfaction, and face challenges with equanimity.

One of the big takeaways from our consulting work is the importance of culture to the success of any kind of strategy initiative. The ability to achieve strategy goals is largely dependent on the culture of the organization—it is an accelerator or a brake. The most successful organizations have the most alignment between the two. Therefore, a powerful and empowering culture is an accelerator on the road to success.

When clients engage The Brooks Group for consulting work, they come to us with what they perceive as a strategy issue that goes beyond developing sales skills. It might be talent strategy, or a go-to-market strategy. But in every case, the culture is an underlying factor in their performance, and it ultimately impacts whether the organization can be successful long term. Yet so often, sales organizations turn to compensation plans and benefits packages in their attempts to entice top salespeople to their companies and "fix problems." And when that does not work, they are at a loss. Nine times out of ten, they are not seeing a cultural problem that exists beneath the surface performance issues.

When the Shoemaker's Children Have No Shoes

> *One of our clients provides training to enterprise organizations—they help their clients improve their organizational culture through more transparent conversations, authentic feedback, and better teamwork. Like many companies in 2020, this organization completely retooled their product offerings and go-to-market strategy due to the pandemic, and their team went permanently remote. But the weight of so much change, happening so quickly, negatively impacted their revenue.*
>
> *In working with them to improve sales, we noticed a cultural disconnect—they, a company in business to improve organizational culture, were not practicing what they preached. Departments were siloed, teamwork was suffering, and many of their sellers were frustrated that the company was not living up to its mission. However, they recognized that improving culture was critical to improving sales. Marketing and sales had to work together to generate leads and win sales. Product development needed sales feedback to guide product enhancements. The company's leadership team intentionally implemented a culture strategy in tandem with their sales strategy, and the organization's financial outlook is improving.*

We will come back to this example shortly, because it illustrates another element of culture that we want to talk more about—agility. Remember we said we would be talking a lot about agility in this book? Stay tuned.

What, Exactly, *Is* Culture?

Cultures can be established by default or by design—they either just happen, or they are intentional. The *most effective* cultures are intentional, created over time, cultivated, and maintained. There's a direct link between culture and outcomes:

- When aligned with strategy and leadership, a strong culture drives positive organizational outcomes.
- Culture can be a powerful differentiator
- Culture guides our interactions with others, and our response to change.

> *One example of an exceptional company culture is the SAS Institute, a North Carolina-based company in Cary. Founded in 1976, the firm has continually received rave reviews from employees and business publications for its unique, beneficial company culture. And SAS has maintained a 45-year streak of profitability, even through the recession of 2008 and the pandemic of 2020-2021.[36] This is a company that understands the essential link between strategy (with innovation in analytics, artificial intelligence, cloud computing, and the Internet of Things) and strong culture.*

A Harvard Business Review article[37] described four attributes of a strong company culture:

- **Shared**—It is in all of us, not one of us (nor the average of all of us, where someone's over-the-top cultural fit makes up for another's lack of cultural fit).
- **Pervasive**—It is seen and unseen at every level, consisting of both visible symbols and mindsets. Think core values on the wall, and also recognition of those who fit the core values.
- **Enduring**—It attracts people who fit in, and those who do not fit in tend to leave.
- **Implicit**—People recognize and respond to it instinctively (including customers and prospective employees, too).

At The Brooks Group, culture has been developed intentionally—our leadership makes purposeful decisions to drive culture, and our core values were created with culture in mind. From there, business decisions are made. For instance, The Brooks Group offers unlimited paid time off (PTO) for our employees. Unlimited PTO reinforces our core value of empowered performance. This idea of core values is essential to any discussion of culture.

Culture and Core Values

Every company has core values, even if they are not written down. If you do not have written values, think about the reasons why people have left (voluntarily and involuntarily). Those reasons are the tangible evidence of the behavioral expectations of people in your company: your company's values.

> *One of our clients, an industrial components supplier, experienced nearly 50% sales employee turnover. They were inconsistent in their strategies— they wanted large OEM customers to purchase their products for production, but the executive management got more excited about a $3,000 custom order for a prototype run than a $300,000 OEM order for manufacturing. They told their field sales teams to go sell to OEMs, but their culture let the inside sales teams withhold information, decide whom to quote, and even who got priority for deliveries. They talked a good game, but did not see their inconsistencies, and it has cost them in repeated turnover at all ranks of the sales team—executive, branch, and account people.*

This is a great example of a clear misalignment between strategy and culture!

Agility and Culture

Now, we alluded to this earlier at the end of our "shoemaker's children" example: The best cultures are not only strong and fit the strategy, but they are adaptable and agile. In fact, organizations with agile cultures earned 15 percent more in annual revenue compared to those in the same industry that were *not* agile.[38]

There was some very interesting research some years back that suggested firms with strong cultures performed well with regard to financial outcomes during stable times, but quite poorly in turbulent environments.[39] At the time, researchers thought this had to do with strong culture ensuring uniform behavior among employees, making it difficult for people to have ideas that challenged norms. But here is what further research found: A culture that has core values around taking initiative, innovating, learning, and so on is far more likely to recognize and adapt to volatile situations.[40]

So, having a strong company culture can execute most effectively on strategies that further its mission and, as a result, be more profitable. But not every culture is created equal. Especially during the recent challenges of 2020–2021, those companies that were able to flex and adapt to change—and even anticipate future change—are those that stayed afloat and prospered.

Building and encouraging an adaptable culture requires that leadership put their focus in several areas:

- **Hiring**—Culture is reflected in hiring. At The Brooks Group, we seek people who fit our culture, and part of the interview process is to determine cultural fit.

- **Curate and Communicate**—Seek and share examples of the culture to reinforce them. When an employee or team takes actions consistent with core values, celebrate it. One of our client's sales teams recognized how hard it was for manufacturing to staff shifts completely during the pandemic, so they worked with management to set up a recognition program for people who worked their shifts and adhered to company policy on COVID safety. The employees saw the company understood the critical nature of their work and responded well to this special recognition.

- **Model the Culture**—From the leadership perspective, model the culture we want to reinforce. Here at The Brooks Group, our sales team models IMPACT by using it daily to engage, understand the objectives of our potential clients, and to recommend solutions that meet their true needs. Many clients have commented that one of the key deciding factors in their choosing to work with The Brooks Group was that we used our own sales methodology.

Sales Leaders Do Not Just Dabble, They Commit to Lasting Cultural Change

Time marches on, buyers are getting younger, and the pandemic showed all of us that we did not have to meet in-person. Buyers of all ages are learning that they are in the driver's seat thanks to the Internet and other technological tools—and they like the control they have. As a direct result, buyers are defining the terms of seller engagement. They can discover all kinds of information about you, your company, your products/services, and reputation without ever being directly in contact with you. They are shortlisting options without sitting through a single sales presentation. This realization is incredibly frustrating for many salespeople, especially those who began selling more than 10 or 15 years ago.

> *The best cultures are not only strong and fit the strategy, but they are adaptable and agile.*

A Gartner webinar reported on the company's research, including the startling statistic that only 20% of B2B sellers believe they are as effective at selling virtually as they are in person.[41] Only a fifth of salespeople surveyed feel they do a good job selling virtually. Clearly, there is a problem: Sales skill development is lagging *way* behind reality. Unfortunately, all too often, the underlying challenge is that sales leadership has been asleep at the wheel, willfully stuck in the status quo, and/or the company culture has not encouraged responsiveness and flexibility.

Not too long ago, we had a regular client come in for some training, and the VP of sales regretfully told us that while they had been doing business with us for ten-plus years, he had recently realized that they "dabbled" in sales training with classes here and there, but never committed to true systemic changes that would enable continuous improvement. This problem is exacerbated by the fact that the industry average for longevity of sales leaders is between eighteen months and two years.

A true commitment to cultural change starts at the executive leadership level. It is communicated to the whole team, and the words are reinforced by action. (Remember earlier when we said that strategy and culture must be aligned?) So executive leadership holds senior sales leadership accountable, who hold frontline sales managers accountable, who hold their sellers accountable for change.

Resiliency comes into play with organizational determination to maintain that commitment. In the example to which we just referred, the client admitted that they were distracted by other priorities that took focus away from sustaining their training. They also indicated that they had allocated a role to reinforcing and sustaining their training, but when that person did not work out in the role (due to cultural fit), they did not fill the role again.

A Good Culture Does Not Fix a Bad Fit (Or a Bad Hire)

Many of our clients recognize they have a performance problem in sales, but rather than take action and replace the individual, they operate on a "bad breath is better than no breath" policy. In most cases, they fear they will have an inability to hire a quality replacement and/or that their low performer will move to a competitor and become a savant salesperson. Sometimes they fear letting a seller go for fear of an empty territory (which probably falls on the manager to cover until a new salesperson is hired).

This has become especially true as VP of Sales roles experience shorter average tenures, so the individual cannot build for the long-term (even if it is only two quarters out) for fear of a single quarterly miss. Much of our Sales Performance Research Center's consulting work is around talent strategy. Not only do we help organizations make better hires, but we help maximize existing talent by aligning individuals to the right roles and right territories, personalize coaching, etc.

Personal Values

Just as organizations have cultures, individuals have motivators—deeply held values that are the *why* behind everything they do. When individuals' motivators are rewarded, they tend to be more engaged, perform better, and express greater job satisfaction. It makes sense that someone who believes at their very core that helping others is the most important thing humans can do would be happy and satisfied in a profession such as nursing, firefighting, homeless relief, or teaching. It also makes sense that someone who is highly motivated by helping people could be a terrific salesperson—if the company they work for has people-first values, the products/services they sell benefit others, and/or they are heavily engaged in customer satisfaction.

(In contrast, they would likely perform badly and/or be miserable in a high-pressure, exceed-quota-at-any-price organization.) That is just one example.

At The Brooks Group, we study six motivators as part of the Brooks Talent Index (BTI). Individuals on every sales team have their own patterns of the relative importance they place on these motivators, which include:

1. **Social Motivator: Sincere, Helping Connectors.** Those who score very high in this motivator have an inherent love of people. What you might observe about the Social person:
   - Has a very strong drive to help others grow professionally
   - Demonstrates a high sincerity factor and caring, helping attitude
   - Has a very high service ethic toward helping others
   - Likes to connect people who have things in common

2. **Aesthetic Motivator: Expressive, Harmonious Creatives.** A higher aesthetic score indicates a relative interest in "form and harmony." What you might observe about the Aesthetic person:
   - Exhibits an appreciation for, and support of, the creative ideas of others
   - Likes rewards based on the results achieved, rather than on the methods used to obtain the results
   - Occasionally prefers some solitary time for personal reflection and rebalancing
   - Seeks form and harmony in experiences and environment
   - Dresses for success—enjoys the latest designer clothes and is always "put together"

3. **Individualistic/Political Motivators: Independent, Leading Influencers.** The primary interest for this individual is power and control. What you might observe about the Individualistic/Political person:
   - Tends to be creative at problem solving with a risk-taking attitude
   - Surprises others with spontaneous ideas or responses
   - Enjoys working in their own way and using their own methods

- Thrives in a team environment but likes freedom in their own work area
- Enjoys work and assignments that give them standing in the eyes of others and evoke respect

4. **Traditional/Regulatory Motivator: Structured, Orderly Rule-Followers.** Individuals with high scores in the Traditional/Regulatory value seek a system (e.g., religious, political, military, or other structure) for living. What you might observe about the Traditional/Regulatory person:
   - Is very structured, orderly, and precise
   - Likes to know how to do something before doing it so it gets done correctly the first time
   - Subscribes to a "rules are made to be followed" position
   - Relies on a sense of security that comes from studying and adhering to procedures and routines
   - Will be very helpful to others who share the same beliefs

5. **Theoretical Motivator: Knowledgeable, Interested Learners.** The primary drivers with the Theoretical motivator are the discovery of knowledge and appetite for learning. What you might observe about the Theoretical person:
   - Has a high degree of curiosity in a wide variety of areas
   - Is often sought out by others on the team to answer questions about projects or procedures
   - Has a strong drive to study their area of interest and expertise to find new ideas, methods, and tools for the team and organization at large
   - Has many interests outside the workplace

6. **Utilitarian/Economic Motivator: Practical, Security Minded "Investors."** Those with a high Utilitarian/Economic value structure show an interest in money and what is useful. What you might observe about the Utilitarian/Economic person:
   - Is interested in what is useful and practical in meeting goals (usually economic ones)

- Is hard-working, competitive, and motivated by financial rewards and challenging compensation plans
- Takes the position that the ends justify the means when profit or project cost/benefits are examined
- Goal-driven, especially financial goals
- Motivated by high pay and attaches importance to high earnings

Consider how the individuals on your sales team might rate these six motivators. Just a few important questions to ask: Is there an individual who clearly stands out as having one or more of these motivators? Does your sales team's ranking match the company culture at your organization? Or does there seem to be a mismatch? How could you ensure your top salespeople feel most rewarded—most *motivated*—by the work they do?

If there is a fit between what an organization values (and, therefore, rewards) and

> *When individuals' motivators are rewarded, they tend to be more engaged, perform better, and express greater job satisfaction.*

what an individual employee values, it can be a match made in heaven. And if your entire team "fit" your company's culture, it's a beautiful thing. Now, let's talk a bit about another important factor in a healthy culture.

The Trust Factor

Remember the old Roadrunner cartoons? Chasing after the Roadrunner, Wile E. Coyote would overtake the bird, only to speed off of a high cliff, legs still circling madly, then—and always a moment too late—he would realize it and then begin the fall. That is how sales professionals sometimes feel once they have won a piece of business and need to hand it off to the customer service, technical, or account management professionals. The salesperson has invested so much time and effort into bringing a great client to the table, and now they have to have enough trust to hand it off to the next part of the team. Unfortunately, they have been burned before; and so often, it is the salesperson who gets the frustrated or angry client call.

We know that historically, there has been a lot of trust missing between inside and outside salespeople, and it's usually the result of a combination of the following factors:

1. Outside salespeople (and sometimes sales leaders) seeing inside folks as glorified administrative assistants—not as partners.
2. An outside salesperson having a "servicer" profile, so they are reluctant to hand off accounts to inside folks.
3. Sales roles have not been clearly defined, and/or people have not been trained well on how to perform handoffs between roles.
4. The wrong people are in the wrong roles or people are being asked to do more than one role.

The good news is that these are all fixable problems.

We are always surprised how easy the trust issue is to solve. Russ worked with a client a couple of years ago whose field sales team felt they had to track every issue due to a lack of trust in the people working inside the plant. Russ said this problem was driven home to him when he took a four-hour drive one day with a Regional VP, who spent the entire time on the telephone following up on the status of very small orders.

When their sales organization was all together for a strategy session, Russ asked, "Is there anyone inside who you do trust?" Slowly, the team began to put names on the white board of people that were good at their job and drove issues to completion. Going forward, these became the key go-to people for the sales team, with a communications agreement that the inside person would give a realistic estimate of when the issue could be closed. Hours of field sales time were returned to productive selling.

Note: The CEO and his management team were in the meeting, and many of the names not listed became areas for performance improvement plans.

Clarity About Roles

At The Brooks Group, we practice what we preach about role clarity and fitting the right person for each role. We have helped countless clients restructure their sales teams to address items 3 and 4 in the list in the previous section, and the results are impressive (if we do say so ourselves).

To get alignment and clarity about roles, first, accurate benchmarks of key positions (including your own) are an absolute necessity. These benchmarks look at the necessary skills, behaviors, and motivations to succeed in the role. Once you have benchmarks, you can review potential applicants or existing people, within the context of the benchmarks to see how well they "fit." Then, assessments made periodically within the workplace give you a snapshot in time of how your people are doing, sales-skill-wise, personal-skill-wise, and attitude-wise. These assessments are also excellent tools for team building and

> *The best cultures are not only strong and fit the strategy, but they are adaptable and agile.*

coaching. Brooks Talent Index (BTI) assessment reports include a look at behaviors (how a person sells or interacts with others—based on DISC measurement) and motivators (why a person performs), as well as emotional intelligence (a person's level of self and social awareness).

Changes Necessitate Communication

Do not deny the reality that your people have changed and that you have changed; your customers also have changed. Even pre-COVID, emotionally impactful events occurred regularly in every person's life, whether it be marriage or divorce or becoming a parent for the first time (or second or third or fourth time). So, a job title might stay the same, but the people themselves shift.

That said, there have been a lot of job shifts in the sales profession, with more specialization of roles from business development through account management. The more that a role has changed from early 2020 to today, the more opportunity there is for stress. If you add that to the general daily life stressors we all have, there is a lot of potential impact on your team. (In fact, we noticed that quite a few salespeople who performed really well during 2020 and early 2021 went hard—and, by the end of 2021, ended up burned out. Makes sense, right?) It is important for you, as a leader, to be able to take the emotional temperature in your organization—for yourself and your employees.

THE BROOKS GROUP

Job Attributes Hierarchy

All human jobs require certain people attributes. This section of the report identifies the composite of the respondents to show which attributes are most important to the job in question. Input from all respondents has been averaged. (Details of individual respondents' input are listed in a later section, JOB ATTRIBUTES COMPOSITE). The graphs below are in hierarchical order, from highest to lowest rankings.

1. Customer Focus - A commitment to customer satisfaction. — 92 VI — 79*

2. Influencing Others - The ability to personally affect others' actions, decisions, opinions or thinking. — 92 VI — 77*

3. Interpersonal Skills - The ability to interact with others in a positive manner. — 86 IMP — 79*

4. Goal Achievement - The overall ability to set, pursue and attain achievable goals, regardless of obstacles or circumstances. — 85 IMP — 74*

5. Resiliency - The ability to quickly recover from adversity. — 85 IMP — 72*

The following scale is used throughout the report.

    0 - 4.9   = NOT IMPORTANT TO JOB
    5.0 - 6.9 = SOMEWHAT IMPORTANT
    7.0 - 8.9 = IMPORTANT
    9.0 - 10 = VERY IMPORTANT

Please note that the population means and standard deviations shown are based on the entire population and are not job/position specific.
* 68% of the population falls within the shaded area.

And, as roles change, communication among team members is more important than ever. Our friend, Tom O'Shea of Agility Consulting & Training, calls it a need for "rampant communications."

Assessments for Cultural Fit

Not only is it important to align individuals to roles and territories, but it is also critical to make sure individuals align with the organizational culture. Are they motivated by what the job rewards? Do they value what the organization values? The assessment tools we use in our consulting not only identify how someone approaches their role, but also their fit to the culture.

Having a selling system that keeps your salespeople laser-focused on the buyer's process is only part of the picture. You can have the most logical, most effective system at the core of your company's sales culture, but if your salespeople aren't suited to the job, your sales quotas will not be met.

If you really want to shift your sales culture, you need to look at the people currently on your team, as well as the people you will be hiring. We have found that the salespeople who can thrive inside of a sales-driven culture have the following:

- **Job Skills**—Product and marketplace knowledge to include experience either in your industry or an industry like yours.
- **Sales Skills**—These are capacities related to a person's capacity to understand and apply state-of-the-art selling skills relative to appropriate levels of prospecting, selling, and account management functions.
- **Personal Skills**—Those individual capacities that determine a person's ability to implement the job and sales skills they possess. These are attributes such as self-starting capacity, self-management, personal motivation, consistency, and literally scores of other essential skills.

More importantly, their combination of these skills match up with your unique cultural environment. That is not to say that you should replace your current sales team because they have the "wrong" instincts. But it might be a good idea to add some new blood. And when you *do* hire new people, look for people who are naturally suited to your new sales environment and the culture you want to build. To do that, use a technique called *behavioral interviewing.* See if they exhibit the qualities that you are looking for. It is a more effective way of vetting new hires than simply looking at their history.

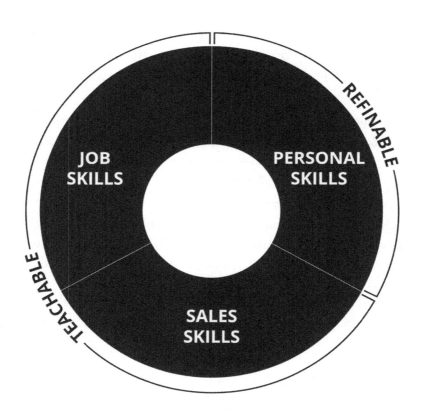

Behavioral Interviewing Pointers

Behavioral interviewing is based on the idea that past performance is a strong indicator of future performance. In behavioral interviews, we ask job candidates about how they have handled specific on-the-job situations.

Examples might include:

Tell us about a time you faced conflict when pursuing a deal. How did you handle it?

Have you ever had to convince a supervisor he or she was wrong about something? How did you approach that?

When work responsibilities have gotten overwhelming and you felt stressed, how did you get through it?

Tell me about the sale or account win you feel most proud of.

Our BTI benchmark reports provide behavioral interviewing questions that are related to the specific job and personal skills required by the job they benchmark.

Once you are sure you have the right people on the bus (or you are in the process of getting there), and they are well trained in a selling system, you can focus on coaching them on the skills of selling that make the difference between average and great performance. In Chapter 9, we are going to draw your attention to the teachable sales principles and skills that will allow your salespeople to become sales guides, or sense-makers, for their prospects as they go along their buying journey.

Ask Yourself the Hard Questions

Start by asking people around the team—what do you think the company values? This becomes a great window into alignment, or lack thereof, of a company's stated and actual values. We advise documenting the values you observe and communicating them clearly across your sales organization. Breathing life into your core values and making them part of your management cadence will help keep your team in alignment, become coaching points themselves, and help with hiring and firing decisions. To get core values entrenched in everything you do as a team requires defining the behavioral expectations for your core values. For example, let's say you describe "excellence" as a core value of your team. But what does that really mean? What does excellence look like in practice? It is much clearer to define it further: "excellence or offering his or her best work on all projects."

Then, the hard part—living up to your values. Again, if excellence is a core value, do you practice it across all sales actions? Are your materials excellent? Are the customer quotations excellent? Does the accuracy and timeliness of customer shipments reflect excellence? It is okay to not be there yet, but you will need to point to specific projects focused on improving excellence for there to be any credibility around that value.

Not sharing your organization's values with your team is a lot like a coach asking a team to play a game without defining the rules. When a team knows the rules, they know what to expect and understand what their role is in getting a win. Part of living up to core values is reinforcing them over time. Recognize people for embodying those core values. Revisit them and remind the team what they mean, and how they should manifest.

Key Takeaways From This Chapter

- Leaders of sales organizations must recognize the influence and importance of their organizational culture, now more than ever, with a large majority of workers reporting that the coronavirus pandemic was the most stressful time of their professional career (even more than 9/11 and the 2008 Great Recession).

- Greater emphasis on collaboration, team-based selling, and the value sales teams bring to their customers necessitates a new approach to company culture—and new attention must be paid to the values behind that culture. "Sales culture" is really the aggregate expectations of individuals about how they will treat customers and be treated as employees.

- What, exactly, a company's core values are matters. An organization that has core values around taking initiative, innovating, learning, and so on is exponentially more able to navigate challenges and change. If your company has a strong culture around agility factors like those, you can execute most effectively on strategies that further your mission and, as a result, be more profitable.

- A true commitment to cultural change starts at the executive leadership level, is communicated to the whole team, and must be reinforced by action consistently over time and across organizational areas.
- Not only is it important to align individuals to roles and territories, but it is also critical to make sure individuals align with the organizational culture. Are they motivated by what the job rewards? Do they value what the organization values?
- Not sharing your organization's values with your team is a lot like a coach asking a team to play a game without defining the rules.

Ask Yourself

- Can you articulate the core values behind your sales organization's culture?
- Why have people quit working for your company? Why have they been fired? (This should tell you something about your organization's values)
- Do you need a better benchmark for whom you need to hire?
- Do you have the best person in place for each role? If not, can you make changes?
- Have you looked at the big-picture system of how a customer interacts with your sales organization? Do you know where are the handoff points? Have you trained your team on the handoffs?
- Has your sales team been trained to adapt to how the buyers to whom they sell change—in terms of equity, diversity, gender, generational, language spoken, etc.?

CHAPTER 4 FREE TOOL
How to Create an Inspired Sales Culture Whitepaper

https://brooksgroup.com/download-tools/

Chapter

5

KPIs and How to Measure Success

Sales performance is considered the easiest area in a company to measure. Revenue. Margin. New logos. Renewals. A few more factors probably come up every time the executive team has a conversation. Sales lives and dies by its key performance indicators (KPIs). And it is inescapable: Those organizations that do focus on KPIs (the right KPIs) to drive their business get great results.

KPIs are also an important part of enabling your sales team and empowering your own great coaching because they allow you to see how your sales reps are performing throughout the entire sales process. The insights gained through tracking KPIs—if chosen intentionally and strategically— can help you determine the tools, training, compensation, and coaching that can help your team as a whole, and individuals specifically, get better results.

We are frequently asked about KPIs, and never more often than during the COVID pandemic, when old measures became ineffective or inappropriate. Few sales leaders have had strong confidence that the KPIs they are using are effective in managing their business. Given this level of curiosity, it seems reasonable to believe sales leaders just don't know what to do about their KPIs in the current environment. We are also seeing that, given that uncertainty, they end up with too many KPIs, too few KPIs, or simply KPIs that are too ineffective.

This lack of confidence shows in our surveys during the pandemic, when organizations were divided between adjusting KPIs and leaving them alone. In Oct 2020, we asked sales organizations whether they had adjusted their KPIs:

- 24% had already implemented changes
- 55% indicated changes were under consideration in 2021
- 21% had no changes planned

We asked the same question again in October 2021. Then:

- 26% had already implemented KPI changes
- 39% indicated changes were under consideration for 2022
- 35% had no changes planned

If your sales organization has undergone any amount of change in the 2020s—especially any of the changes we are talking about in this book—then it is worth evaluating your existing KPIs. Otherwise, your activities may not be providing accurate data for decision making, and they may not be driving the activity you need from your sales team. We can say with absolute confidence that those organizations that focus on the right KPIs drive their business to get great results.

So what *are* the right KPIs? Well, it depends greatly on your industry, your business, your goals, and your salespeople's quotas and capacities. The best KPIs for your sales team are the ones that measure a key behavior you want to influence in your salespeople. (Note to self: Just because you can measure something does not mean it is an effective KPI.)

> *Russ worked for a company that measured average time of a customer support telephone call, and the executive management team told the Director of Customer Support to reduce the call times in order to reduce the wait for customers in the telephone queue. Within a week, times came down. The downside was that there was an offsetting increase in the return of units determined to be "no trouble found." Rather than fully troubleshoot the customer issue, support staff would more quickly ask the customer to return the unit and ship out a replacement. KPI achieved, business results suffered.*

Effective KPIs usually drive key components of a sales or company goal and provide a way for the members of your team to benchmark their performance against their peers.

Lessons from High-Growth Companies

High-growth companies do things differently from their peers—that is no secret—and, as we have been showing you, the ones that survive and thrive in the face of all kinds of economic and societal ups and downs are the ones that adapt to change. One thing we would like to draw your attention to is what changes they are making relative to KPIs that are really putting them on track to grow faster than their peers.

ZS Associates published a study in October 2020 in which they reported the results of a survey of more than 200 middle market executives across several industries.[42] For the survey, they identified what they called a high-growth cohort, which demonstrated a revenue growth rate of at least 15% over the past three years, and they measured those organizations against a lower growth cohort out of the same industry.

One of the key findings was that the high-growth organizations were measuring different KPIs than their counterparts (but roughly the same number of KPIs—23 versus 21). (Though we would suggest that a better number for any one department is 4-8, which can easily be remembered by a department's personnel). In addition, they were reviewing them and adapting them more frequently and sharing them across their organizations on a wider basis. Sounds like *agility*, doesn't it?

We have taken a look at what the high performers did differently:

- First, the high-growth companies **curated their KPIs.** By that, we mean they boiled down what the most important factors are to reach their business objectives. Sure, that sounds like common sense, but as with most things that seem commonsensical, lots of folks do not do them! The high-growth firms looked precisely at what their organizations were trying to achieve, and they are tracking that in terms of KPIs—no more, no less.

- Next, roughly half of those high-growth companies had **tracked *new* KPIs** within the last year. That means they are actively engaged in assessing the KPIs they track to be sure they are truly useful in achieving the results required by their company's or business unit's objectives. They were more likely to adopt new KPIs and abandon those that were not useful: While 50% of those high-growth companies had tracked new KPIs in the last year, only 34% of the lower growth companies did.

- The high-growth all-stars also **revisit their KPIs regularly**; they have a standard cadence for going back, looking at their metrics and determining whether they need to be adjusted. Eighty percent of the high-growth companies in this survey evaluate their KPIs on a yearly basis, and about 25% of those also review them even more frequently (such as on a quarterly basis). So, particularly if you are in a fast-changing environment like most all of us have been in for the last few years, but also if you have a seasonal business or aggressive growth goals, it may be worth your time to set regular KPI reviews more frequently.

- Fourth, high-growth companies **used what we call calculated KPIs**—metrics that take multiple data points and shape them into a single metric. These were always a small percentage of their overall KPIs, but they were used when a clear relationship was established between different data. They make sure they are easy to understand and lead to clear decisions. For example, 50% of the high-growth companies track customer lifetime value as a metric. In contrast with just tracking average customer spend (single data point), customer lifetime value factors in lifetime spend, purchase frequency, and maybe even how long customers stay with you. These multiple data points can provide a more nuanced view of what is going on in your business, particularly if you are looking at your overall customer acquisition costs, how to target your marketing spend, and which customers to track or target. (Other examples of calculated KPIs would be tracking win rate or pipeline advance rates.)

> *The best KPIs for your sales team are the ones that measure a key behavior you want to influence in your salespeople.*

- Last, the high-growth companies **use KPIs to connect their organizations**; in other words, they communicate their KPIs clearly across different departments. The average high-growth company in the study shared 12 KPIs with their sales reps, in contrast to eight KPIs that the lower growth companies shared with their sales teams. Thirty-two percent of those were KPIs such as shared value and volume of opportunities across pipeline stages—the kind of thing that can bring sales reps together and understand the impact that they are having on the larger organization beyond just their own individual numbers. The higher performing sales organizations also shared team-wide KPIs with their organizations as a whole to show their impact on the organization. Other shared KPIs to consider might be customer satisfaction or net promoter scores. (We also recommend a shared scorecard between sales and marketing, tracking leads by source and pipeline velocity.)

Clearly, the high-growth firms are paying close attention to consistently reviewing not just the numbers associated with the KPIs they track, but also evaluating the metrics themselves to ensure they are truly in support of achieving results. KPIs cannot be a "set it and forget it" tool. Ideally, they drive alignment between departments, promote transparency within the organization, and inform company-wide business conversations. All of those factors play significantly into an organization's ability to be agile and take advantage of surprising opportunities and weather major challenges.

> *Recently we worked with a client to re-baseline their KPIs. We started by asking a broad group of salespeople what they believed drove their results. Then we started sorting through the ideas, combining and looking for which might be metrics that drove the other metrics (keystone KPIs—see the next section).*
>
> *Our client had been in business for many years, and in the last decade had gotten orders from nearly all of the potential customers in their markets. So, we zeroed in on two key drivers of business—accounts that in the previous year had purchased a large amount of product, but were buying at a significantly lower rate this year; and customers that had not made significant purchases in the last three years. By refocusing on these two customer categories, they found better focus building sustainability in their customer base, and sustainability in their revenue growth.*

Keystone KPIs

Have you heard of keystone habits? The term was coined by Charles Duhigg, author of *The Power of Habit*, and it describes specific habits—good ones—that have the power to transform your life. The basic idea behind keystone habits is that if you make one small change in one area, that change will lead to other positive changes. In other words, what are those leverage points that you have that ensure you move in the direction you want to be heading and possibly accelerate your progress there.

For example, research has shown that if you have a morning routine—you get up and do the same thing every morning—that that allows you to show up at the office with more organized thoughts, you end up more productive at work, which helps you have better health, and end up happier. One study showed that people who lay their gym clothes out at night have a far greater likelihood of putting on those clothes to jog or head to the gym in the morning. Even making your bed can be a keystone habit—believe it or not, it has been shown that there is a correlation between making your bed and having good budgeting skills!

This principle should help you focus the KPIs you choose for your organization. What are those things—a fairly small number of them—that start to push us in the right direction toward being more effective sales professionals?

How Many of Your Leads Are from Referrals?

One of the keystone KPIs we recommend tracking is the source of new opportunities. When you are trying to find new leads and it is a real struggle, an important metric to track is how many leads are coming from referrals. Are your customers helping you find new business? Referrals is a low-cost metric to track—all you have to do is flag how many leads come from customers. In addition, a greater proportion of leads coming from referrals has two advantages:

1. Referrals are the easiest business to convert from opportunity to close because the trust that they have in the relationship that already exists gets transferred for you as the seller.
2. Referrals are also a measure of true customer satisfaction because they tell you that your customers like you enough to refer you out to other people that they know in their industry.

Statistics show that more than 90% of customers would give a referral, but somewhere less than 15% of sales people ever ask for one. Selling to existing customers is the most efficient way of increasing revenue for your organization. That is why it is critical that you keep an eye on customer service and the performance indicators involved with it.

Customer Satisfaction KPIs

Customer satisfaction is something most companies strive to achieve, but find hard to measure. Surveys that ask, "How satisfied are you?" are usually ineffective because research shows that people who are unhappy respond to surveys much more than those who are happy. Think about it? What inspires you to write a review? A good experience— especially if it is expected—or a bad experience. What we've found is that measuring secondary factors, such as the three noted below, are much more effective in understanding how satisfied your customers truly are.

1. *Existing client engagement*
2. *Retention and churn rates*
3. *Customer lifetime value*

How Often Are Your Salespeople Directly Interacting with Prospects and Customers?

A McKinsey study found that high-performing salespeople spent 22% more of their week in front of customers, communicating directly with them (this could mean a telephone call, video call, or an in-person meeting).[43] So another thing that we recommend measuring is how often your salespeople are really on the phone or face-to-face (either virtual or in-person) with prospects and customers versus how much time they doing other things such as paperwork, traveling, or sitting in internal meetings. McKinsey's research also found that those top salespeople who spent more time in front of customers produced four times as much revenue as the lowest producing salespeople.

Maddy Osman of Cirrus Insight writes in a blog post about "conversational intelligence" as what we would call a keystone KPI. She describes conversational intelligence as "engaging others by creating shared personal connections rooted in developing trust and fostering a collaborative environment."[44] Sounds a lot like personalized experiences enabled by a focus on trust and value, right? Tracking it requires looking into how effectively your salespeople are communicating with prospects and clients, measuring conversation progress over time.

Gartner reported in September 2021 that when salespeople take the time to learn what a customer values and communicates how their solution is superior to competitive offerings, the likelihood of a high-quality purchase with no regret for the buyer is just over 50% greater.[45] This outcome will drive higher customer satisfaction and referral rates. The keystone KPI is likely "how clearly a salesperson can articulate to their sales management the unique rather than generic value they bring to this prospect." Sales managers can "grade" the explanation as low, average, or high; and you can measure the win rates at each of these levels, the percentage of understanding by each salesperson, or even time-to-close from proposal to commitment for each level.

Are Your Salespeople Outbound-Focused or Inbound-Focused?

On what type of accounts should your sales teams be focusing? Most sales and company executives will say they want new customers—to grow market share by winning at an ever increasing rate. In our sales management programs we will often ask, "If you were a salesperson for your company, how much time would you spend prospecting for new business?" A number around 70% is usually the average. However, ask that same question of their salespeople, and a number more like 20% surfaces. (And then when asked to confirm that they really do spend the equivalent of one full day a week prospecting for new business, the number declines to 5%-10%, which translates into two to four hours a week.)

Why the big difference? Two key areas:

1. **Most salespeople have responsibility for existing and new accounts.** When we look at the way they are compensated, the cost of losing an account is usually much greater than the benefit of winning a new one. So, dollars and cents drive them to spend more time on existing accounts.

2.   **Organizations have reduced the amount of support a salesperson has over the last few decades.** Reporting, expenses, proposal development, not to mention internal meetings all consume an increasing amount of a salesperson's time. Ever give direction to your sales team about needing to increase new prospect selling without letting them spend less time in the CRM or other reporting? Ever cancel your weekly sales call for a month so they can spend the time searching for new accounts?

What Are Your Salespeople's Conversion Rates at Each Step of the Sales Process?

For you as a sales leader, always remember that the sales funnel and the sales process are both critical. Every sales leader wants a smooth funnel that totals some multiple of your actual target.

Yet the keystone KPI is likely based on conversion rates at each phase of the sales process. For example, are marketing-qualified leads converting at only a small percentage when compared to sales-initiated leads? What can be tuned to get better marketing leads? If opportunities are moving through the sales process only to be hung up at the close, is there some activity or content that is needed to be able to move the opportunity to closed?

Some of the most powerful, actionable information you can observe is looking at how many opportunities and the aggregate (or average) value your salespeople have at each step of the sales process. This simple exercise tells you if your entire team is on plan with enough qualified prospects in each step of the sale, as well as if each salesperson is on track to meet their personal quota. It also allows you to track where in the sales process individual salespeople seem not to be reaching expected milestones or conversion rates.

> *Statistics show that more than 90% of customers would give a referral, but somewhere less than 15% of sales people ever ask for one.*

What are your conversion averages when you go from lead to opportunity to proposal to close? For example, look at your best salesperson, your average salesperson, and your lowest performer. If each one of them can make a small—even 4% or 5%—improvement in the conversion rate from lead to opportunity, it's going to have a significant impact on your top and bottom lines.

Metrics that focus on the sales funnel or sales cycle present excellent opportunities to see where your salespeople are doing great and where they are facing challenges. These leading indicators will help you intervene with coaching where it is necessary. Here are some examples of KPIs related to pipeline health:

- Marketing-qualified leads
- Sales-qualified leads
- Appointments set
- Open opportunities
- Presentations
- Proposals generated

You should be clear with your reps that tracking sales activities is not about inspecting their every move. There is a big difference between reviewing the sales funnel and trying to understand how they are moving opportunities through the funnel. Understanding how your team members are performing will help you tighten up the sales process and get closer to achieving revenue goals—which is a win-win for everyone. And if you know where they are coming up short, then you can coach or take other actions to help them get back on track before there is a miss.

Here are some examples of KPIs related to sales rep efficiency:

- Close won/Close lost rates
- Length of sales cycle
- Upsell/Cross-sell rates
- Quota attainment
- Average cost per lead
- Conversion rate

We do recognize that for some organizations the time between first contact with an opportunity and the close of the opportunity is too short to measure in a sales funnel. In that case, the emphasis should be on

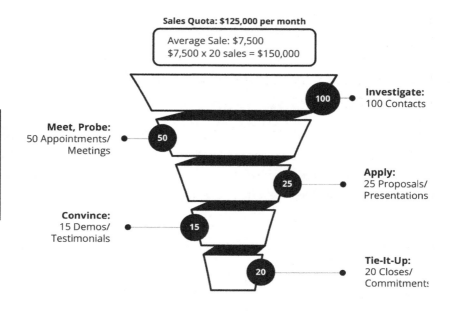

HEALTHY

Sales Quota: $125,000 per month

Average Sale: $7,500
$7,500 x 20 sales = $150,000

Investigate:
100 Contacts — 100

Meet, Probe:
50 Appointments/
Meetings — 50

Apply:
25 Proposals/
Presentations — 25

Convince:
15 Demos/
Testimonials — 15

Tie-It-Up:
20 Closes/
Commitments — 20

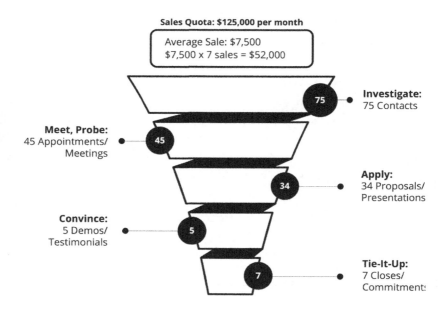

UNHEALTHY

Sales Quota: $125,000 per month

Average Sale: $7,500
$7,500 x 7 sales = $52,000

Investigate:
75 Contacts — 75

Meet, Probe:
45 Appointments/
Meetings — 45

Apply:
34 Proposals/
Presentations — 34

Convince:
5 Demos/
Testimonials — 5

Tie-It-Up:
7 Closes/
Commitments — 7

number of leads generated and average time to close for the team and specific salesperson. Metrics such as upsell/cross-sell or average sales amount might also come into play.

Is Your Organization Retaining and Managing Accounts Profitably?

"Reality is the 80/20 rule" usually holds here: 80% of your company's future revenue will come from just 20% of your existing customers. It is far more profitable to retain existing customers than to find new ones, so it is key that your team keep customer satisfaction top of mind.

- Retention rate
- Customer churn
- Customer satisfaction score
- Support requests
- Support calls
- Support emails
- Time to resolution
- Product engagement

In order to recognize new business opportunities—and be seen as trusted advisors when making recommendations—your account managers and sales staff must demonstrate their value to the client. This requires staying on top of each key account and making sure the customer feels supported and confident in working with your organization. Performance indicators for strengthening relationships include:

- Strategic conversations—number of calls or meetings where a business topic not directly related to a purchase of your product is discussed.
- Referrals
- Participation in your customer events and activities

In the end, the goal of your account management effort is to increase revenue. For that reason, it is important to measure growth with key indicators or performance measures that might include:

- Customer upsell revenue
- Customer cross-sell revenue
- Contract extension revenue

Establishing Your Sales Team's KPIs

Remember, your KPIs should be based on asking what behavior you want to encourage, whether it is your prospect's, your customer's, or your sales team's. Once you determine what potential outcomes have the most value for your organization, you will need to determine what, exactly, to measure to get the insight you need.

My prospect/customer/team as a whole needs to...	A solid KPI to track would be...

When selecting your list of KPIs, do not go overboard: **Less is more**. It can be tempting to track every data point related to the sales department, but the most important information will be lost if you try to track too much. Too many KPIs cause frustration for the sales team, too, and it does not help drive high-gain activities for sellers. One of our consulting clients has set too many KPIs for their sales team, resulting in frustration and stagnation in the sales team, rather than driving the right or most important activities. Keep the total number of KPIs you are tracking to eight or fewer to make your meeting scorecard or sales dashboard easy to understand at a glance.

Many sales organizations focus all of their KPIs on "end-process" measurements, such as opportunity-to-win ratio and revenue (or margin) per salesperson. These black-and-white measurements do not foster growth in a sales force and only reveal the end result, not where the opportunities for coaching and improvement exist. Instead, we recommend relying more heavily on "in-process" measurements such as appointments booked or number of demos given, which allow you to coach your reps while they are working toward their sales goals. The leading indicators you choose will be unique to your team and the objectives that need to be met: Make sure that you are tracking the specific sales activities that will empower your team to achieve their goals.

Connecting KPIs to Compensation

As we have said, KPIs are an essential tool for measurement—they drive organizational decisions and inform coaching—and KPIs drive the desired seller behavior. After all, what gets measured, gets done. Ideally, your incentive structure also drives the desired behavior. So, what's the right incentive structure for your organization?

In places such as a *Harvard Business Review* article[46], authors and experts are indicating that now might be the time to eschew individual incentives in favor of a bonus plan based on company-wide performance. While we agree that sales incentive plans should be tweaked to adapt to changing environments, and a more supportive and collaborative approach is definitely useful, we believe that individual incentives also still play a critical role.

In Defense of Individual Financial Incentives

Simply put, compensation drives behavior. Of course, team- or organization-wide incentives certainly can encourage participation and collaboration and allow for company-wide celebration of milestones reached. But there is nothing more impactful than a direct connection between an individual's performance and the rewards they receive.

If you have established clear expectations of each person in your extended sales organization, your team will know exactly what they are responsible for and what success looks like. If you have involved your team in setting performance expectations and the deliverables that signify achievement, it seems reasonable that you should offer financial incentives for those achievements. That is especially true for sales organizations that have historically been built on the "coin operated" model—the most common rewards for salespeople have been financial.

In Favor of Team Incentives

We have talked a bit about the "new" team selling that many companies are engaging in elsewhere in this book, describing how the inside-outside sales dichotomy is quickly becoming obsolete in many industries. Marketing personnel and "inside" sales representatives both play important roles in dealing with prospective buyers. Customer service professionals often interact with client personnel more frequently than "outside" sales representatives do. The traditional titles and tasks we associate with the sales team no longer reflect what is really happening as buyers become more and more independent and opinionated.

With buying by committee being so pervasive now, and CxO involvement in the buying process (especially finance) the norm, your sales team has many additional possible touchpoints during the sales process. Consequently, there are more people within your organization who may need to interface with folks in the buyer's organization—whether it is your CFO meeting with the buyer's CFO or a buyer end-user representative meeting with your technical design specialist. It just makes sense to incentivize a wider range of employees to reinforce the value of collaboration over individual achievement. There are many forward-thinking companies out there that are incentivizing non-sales personnel, including tying a meaningful portion of each employee's pay to annual business results.

> *Recently we worked with a software company that takes this approach. While there is a small financial commission plan for salespeople, more significant is the company wide bonus plan, paid quarterly for performance. While this approach will not work for every company, it has helped them grow consistently for over a decade.*

The burden with team incentive plans is the need for clearly defined roles, well understood metrics, and a commitment of all participants to be a part of the team (all three of which likely are functions of your sales culture).

We believe you can measure KPIs that are both team- and individual-focused, and then tie them to compensation and other incentives. Here are a few examples that might be good for your dashboard:

KPI	Team, Individual, or Both?	Relevant Compensation/ Incentive
New logo revenue	Team or individual	Usually a commission tied to revenue amount
Customer renewals/ additional purchases	Team or individual	Bonus based on renewal or returning customer rates
Marketing to sales leads conversion	Individual	Monthly bonus upon achieving desired levels
Sales referrals	Individual	Bonus based on milestones for entering the lead

KPIs for Agility

For all the buzz that "agility" gets as a focal point in discussions about business success, it is not necessarily a simple thing to measure directly. In general, organizations trying to measure it usually default to some version or another of "taking less time to get better outcomes." Some of the best measures we have seen include:

- *Trend of revenue per employee over time (measured quarterly or monthly over a few years—how is the trend)*
- *"Creativity used to solve my problem" metric taken from customer surveys*
- *Revenue from products introduced in the last n time period. (where n = 2x or 3x your typical sales cycle)*
- *Presentation in sales and/or company meetings on key learnings from customer or new skills learned by the employee in a quarter*

Key Takeaways from This Chapter

1. Sales leaders just do not know what to do about their KPIs in the current environment and, given that uncertainty, they end up doing nothing. (This is bad.) Well-chosen KPIs can drive exceptional results; poorly chosen ones can have unintended consequences that add a lot of stress and little value.

2. High-growth organizations measure different KPIs than their counterparts, review them and adapt them more frequently, and share them across their organizations on a wider basis. They pay close attention to consistently reviewing not just the numbers associated with the KPIs they track, but also evaluating the metrics themselves to ensure they are truly in support of achieving results.

3. The best KPIs for your sales team are the ones that measure key behaviors you want to influence. This may be for your salespeople, your sales team, or your customers. (Note to self: Just because you can measure something does not mean it is an effective KPI.)

4. Ideally, KPIs drive alignment between departments, promote transparency within the organization, and inform company-wide business conversations. KPIs such as shared value and volume of opportunities across pipeline stage can bring sales reps together and understand the impact that they are having on the larger organization— the same data should be shared company wide.

Ask Yourself

-   What are the big-picture goals for your sales team in terms of end results, in-process milestones met, growth, and culture? Have you communicated those goals clearly to your team?

-   Do the KPIs you have in place encourage results? Do you need to recalibrate any KPIs to help drive your team to better or different results?

-   How recently have you reviewed and revised the KPIs you are tracking?

-   How does your incentive plan take into consideration individual performance and team performance?

- If you are not already doing so, can you work with your peers to establish KPIs between departments?

CHAPTER 5 FREE TOOL
Monthly Quota Reality Check

https://brooksgroup.com/download-tools/

Chapter
6

Sales Teams Must Be Agile, Not Fragile

According to the Harvard Business Review, there are four things that sales organizations must do to adapt to crisis.[47] In particular, the authors reviewed changes in selling and explored the types of sales roles that might be needed in the future. The overall point was that increased digital selling is here to stay in some form or fashion, and that organizations may be rethinking the size of their teams, the expectations for success, and other factors based on that prediction.

Our own anecdotal experience agrees. We have seen that the most stable, profitable organizations made some quick pivots during the COVID pandemic, and it is clear that some of the adaptations they had to make were more beneficial than the practices, processes, and technologies they replaced. Interestingly, though, only about half of the organizations we surveyed in mid-2020 reported that they were likely to make changes coming out of the pandemic environment: 31% said they were "extremely likely," and 20% said they were "somewhat likely" to change the size of their sales teams. Similarly, in terms of the types of sales roles that we are seeing, only about half of the organizations we surveyed were likely to make changes to the sales role, with 25% "somewhat likely," and 23% "extremely likely."

For us, the percentage of firms that were anticipating change was disappointingly low. Half of folks we surveyed were not anticipating making changes in response to a global pandemic environment. There was a real opportunity for people to think about what they do and how they can do it better. Instead, 50% of them just were not even considering it.

In 2021, we repeated the survey, and the results were interesting:

- Nearly three-quarters of respondents had already increased the size of their sales teams or were considering an increase for 2022.
- Thirty-five percent had already realigned sales territories, and another 30% were considering this change for 2022.

If we convince you of nothing else in this book, we hope we are convincing you that change usually requires change. When the world changes, sales organizations must change along with it. The most successful companies are able to have resilient teams that are capable of making rapid, intelligent shifts in response to changes in everything from a specific customer's demands to an entire industry.

Opportunities to Recalibrate and Grow

There has been quite a bit of research since the 2008 financial crisis, with studies attempting to uncover what strategies were most successful and what decisions proved to be most and least successful—and especially, how the actions taken during a financial downturn impact results during the recovery. The companies that were able to survive and thrive in spite of the crisis can teach us lessons today as we attempt to weather the COVID pandemic and prepare for the next global crisis. And two of the most common attributes of winners are agility and resiliency.

It is pretty clear that the companies that are still around used that financial crisis as a chance recalibrate and rethink some of their business practices. The ones that did tended not just to rebound faster but also to overall gain market share in the two years following the crisis.[48]

Agility Must Be Practiced

When the U.S. Army was preparing folks at the Army War College to be sent to the Middle East in the 1990s, training materials described strategic leadership in the context of a VUCA world: volatile, uncertain, complex, and ambiguous. Tom O'Shea of Agility Consulting takes that construct and brings it to the modern day. His recent surveys consistently show more than 90% of business leaders predicting more volatility and ambiguity over the next three years, and 80% predicting more uncertainty and complexity. Seventy-five percent of respondents say they "need improvement in anticipating change."

It is a fact that while we have more access to data than ever, the volatility we have been seeing in the world—across markets and industries—has challenged our forecasting ability. If you cannot look ahead with confidence, you must be able to ensure that your organization can respond rapidly and assertively to variability and opportunities. To make that happen, agility must be a cultural construct, built into the structure and operations of the sales team—from a corporate culture of change receptivity and KPIs that are established to evaluate progress, to the sales team organizational structure and the pay plans used to reward salespeople.

Sequoia Capital, one of the most successful American venture capital firms, survived the crisis of 2008 by continuing to make investments, not cutting spending. Then-partner Greg McAdoo told *The Wall Street Journal* in 2009, Sequoia's position was that "recessions reward discipline." As he put it:

> "...a lot of startups got going in good times and frankly fell into bad habits you would not get into in a bad economy but can kill you now. The message was not to fold up your tents but to reevaluate...and re-engineer your business." [49]

While a lot of years passed, the company stayed true to that philosophy. In March 2020, Sequoia published their advice for surviving the COVID-19 crisis.[50] The advice included thinking carefully about every aspect of corporate spending and taking proactive steps to address the crisis at hand, then concluded:

> "Having weathered every business downturn for nearly fifty years, we've learned an important lesson—nobody ever regrets making fast and decisive adjustments to changing circumstances... In some ways, business mirrors biology. As Darwin surmised, those who survive 'are not the strongest or the most intelligent, but the most adaptable to change.'"

We love both quotes, for obvious reasons. Sales teams have changed—or need to—and they need to keep on changing in response to their environments. Change cannot be something you are forced to do because you must make changes or shutter your business. Change must be expected, anticipated, and embraced.

Your customers are showing their own agility by changing their buying processes to minimize risk and ensure purchases align with or advance larger strategic initiatives. Sellers must also understand and adapt to these processes to out of necessity. Three big changes we have identified where your sellers need to become more adept are: selling to committees, working with purchasing/procurement, and selling to the C-suite.

In addition, we have seen that the 2020s have influenced changes in what buyers expect from their vendors (see Chapter 2), and how they want to experience the sales process. The most successful sales organizations will adapt to these expectations, even if it means reorganizing their own structures to deliver a better customer experience and capture every opportunity.

Team Buying

C-suite involvement in decision-making has increased dramatically over the last few years, especially during the COVID pandemic. There are many reasons why (and we will cover some of those in just a bit), but with so much uncertainty about the future in many industries, it is a trend that seems ready to hang around. As we have mentioned in earlier chapters, there have been reasons why purchasing/procurement became a key player in the decision-making process, especially since the Recession of 2008. And it is clear that consensus decision-making involving various stakeholders is de rigueur in today's complex and/or costly B2B purchases.

Who Influences Buying Decisions?

In all but the tiniest businesses, buying decisions are made by some sort of formal or informal group. The formal structure of an organization is the official way the company works—think about your company's organizational chart. But there are always informal structures in organizations, no matter how large or small. The informal structure is how the organization really works. For example, the purchasing manager may be influenced by an engineer he knows, likes, and trusts to purchase a particular technical brand; or a midlevel VP may pressure him to source items from a favored corporate partner.

As team consensus buying decisions involving multiple layers of B2B organizations—either driven by or actively involving higher and higher levels of management—become the norm, the salesperson's job becomes more challenging, does it not? Do not worry, though. We have a variety of tools that will help your sales team get focused on the right people with the right messages at the right time.

In general, it is helpful to think of your prospect's decision-making team in terms of the roles they usually play:

- **Gatekeeper:** Every salesperson's least favorite (or most favorite) challenge, whose role is all too often misinterpreted as to keep you away from the real source(s) of power. This could be anyone (or multiple people) from receptionists to purchasing specialists. The reality is a gatekeeper's key role is to only let the brightest and best to access her or his boss. Gatekeepers are the first point of selling, not an obstacle to hammer through.

- **User:** This is the person who benefits directly from the products or services you sell. If you sell bearings, it is the person who is responsible for installing the bearings into the company's products. Or maybe it is the factory manager who gets the benefit of longer lasting bearings. If you sell accounting software, it is the accounts receivable and accounts payable team.

- **Decision Maker:** This is the individual (or individuals) with the ultimate authority to say yes or no. This may be the person whose budget the purchase will be allocated to, or perhaps a Senior Executive, Board, or Executive Committee who must sign off on expenditures.

- **Influencer:** Influencers have sway over the purchase decision, but they are not the ultimate decision maker, user, or gatekeeper. Ideally, influencers are your internal advocates, but they could be advocates for a competitor instead. (This role often appears in complex sales environments; your clients may or may not have individual[s] in the role.)

- **Internal Advocate:** Ideally, you have more than one Internal Advocate on your side within your prospect/client organization. They will likely give assistance as you navigate the corporate maze of policies, procedures, and personnel. They usually provide subtle (or not-so-subtle) direction on the decision-making process on your behalf.

We will talk more about how to approach the various individuals in key roles who influence buying decisions in a moment. We cannot emphasize enough, though, the importance of taking the time to map out the various stakeholders involved in both the formal and informal structures of prospects' and clients' organizations. Sales professionals have many excellent opportunities to become part of the decision-making process by educating and influencing folks across the organization, contributing valuable insights and knowledge in a variety of appropriate ways.

The Contact Map

A Contact Map can help you uncover buying patterns, formal and informal decision-making structures, and motives for each individual touchpoint you have within the organization. Here is how to do it:

1. Draw the reporting structure for the organization.
2. Put influencers' names and titles in each box.
3. Draw a line from any person who influences another person to the person (or people) they influence. Do not forget outside influencers.
4. Make an educated guess about what each individual's primary Buyer Style is: Dominance, Influence, Steadiness, or Compliance. (See chapter 8 for definitions)
5. Make note of the role that each plays in the decision-making process: User, Influencer, Decision Maker, Advocate, or Gatekeeper. Some people may have more than one role.
6. Describe their level of influence: high, medium, or low.
7. Describe how much credibility you have with each person: high, medium, or low.
8. Make a reasonable guess about their preference/bias: Favors us, neutral, favors alternative.
9. Write the initials of whom within your organization "owns" the relationship with each person on your map.

1: Behavior Style

D □   **I** □   **S** □   **C** □
(Dominance) (Influence) (Steadiness) (Compliance)

2: Role the Individual Plays

U □   **I** □   **D** □   **A** □   **G** □
(User) (Influencer) (Decision Maker) (Advocate) (Gatekeeper)

3: Level of Influence

H □   **M** □   **L** □
(High)   (Medium)   (Low)

4: Level of Credibility

H □   **M** □   **L** □
(High)   (Medium)   (Low)

5: Preference / Bias

+ □   **N** □   **-** □
(Favors us) (Neutral) (Favors Alternative)

6: Relationship Owner

_____

(Use individual's initials)

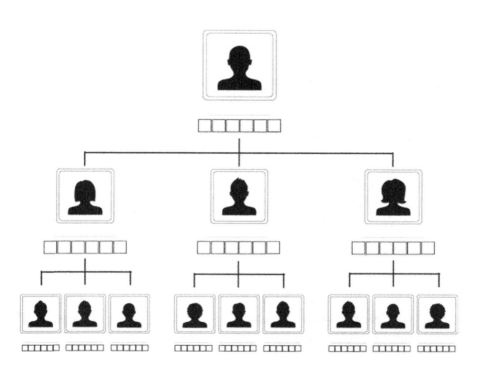

Almost every time we have seen a salesperson or team attempt to complete a Contact Map, it has significant gaps. That is why it is such a fantastic tool. Anywhere you see a gap is a place you will be well served by uncovering additional information—you may uncover surprising connections and insights. At the very least, a Contact Map helps you look carefully at an account and ensure that your sales team are, themselves, influencing the right people.

The Decision Pyramid

Every contact you have within a prospect or customer's organization falls somewhere on what we depict as the Decision Pyramid. This is a helpful tool because it indicates your contact's primary focus in terms of strategy, results, and/or outcomes. To engage contacts at each of these levels, we must tailor our conversations, marketing messages, sales tools, and other communications to their areas of focus.

In the first example here (Figure 1), we have filled in some key roles that exist in a fairly typical traditional manufacturing enterprise. At the top are titles such as CEO, President, and Owner; in the middle are roles such as Plant Manager, Engineering, and Quality Manager; and, at the lowest level on the pyramid, are Operators and Purchasing Agents.

For a hospital (Figure 2), the top level is comprised of the key officers in the carpeted parts of the hospital—CEO, COO, Chief Medical Officer. Layer 2 incorporates Supply Chain Directors, Director of Nursing, Department Heads, and specific clinical experts—surgeons, etc. Layer 3 includes many staff roles, especially nurses in the operating rooms or patient care, along with support groups such as purchasing or security. Over the last decade, hospitals have been utilizing Value Analysis Committees (VAC) that receive input from all of the clinical personnel at Layers 2 and 3, then review and make purchasing decisions. The VAC is composed of Layer 1 and Layer 2 individuals.

This hierarchy of decision making is even visible in fairly simple purchase transactions—for example, building trades. Layer 1 would be the owner or General Contractor executives, Layer 2 is project managers and construction supervisors, and Layer 3 is comprised of the tradespeople and purchasing. If the decision is to buy one brand or another of a commodity, Layers 2 and 3 can make the decision. However, if the supplier has a value

Figure 1: Typical Manufacturing Decision-Maker Roles

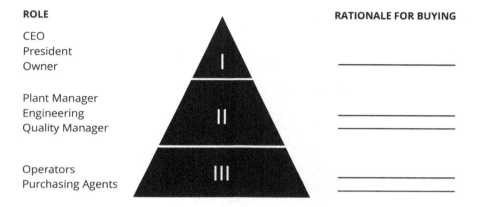

ROLE

CEO
President
Owner

Plant Manager
Engineering
Quality Manager

Operators
Purchasing Agents

RATIONALE FOR BUYING

Figure 2: Typical Hospital Decision-Maker Roles

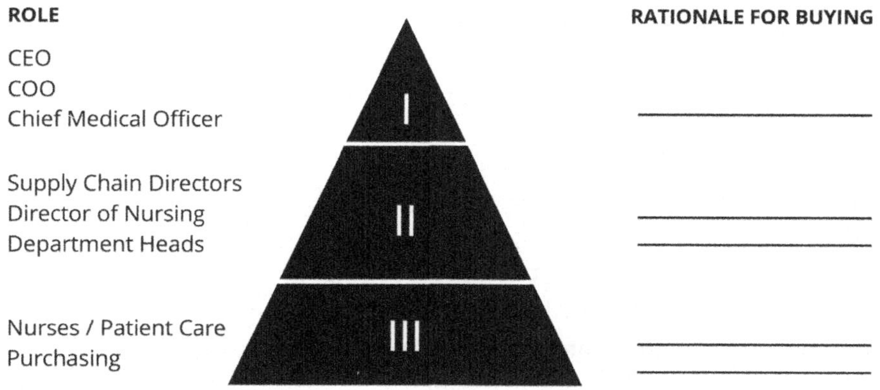

ROLE

CEO
COO
Chief Medical Officer

Supply Chain Directors
Director of Nursing
Department Heads

Nurses / Patient Care
Purchasing

RATIONALE FOR BUYING

proposition that is broader than just a material, say, special fabrication or other labor-saving services, they will typically have to introduce the "higher unit price, but overall project savings" proposal to Layers 1 and 2.

Figure 3: Typical Building Trades Decision-Maker Roles

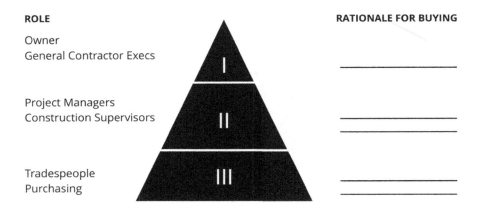

ROLE

Owner
General Contractor Execs

Project Managers
Construction Supervisors

Tradespeople
Purchasing

RATIONALE FOR BUYING

Depending on your company's product or service type, complexity of sale, unique sales roles, and other factors, your typical prospect's Decision Pyramid may or may not resemble any of the examples we have presented. The essential point we want to emphasize is that conversations *must* be tailored to the right level and appeal to the buyer's rationale at that level. In the next few sections, we are going to look more deeply into some of the core decision-making roles we are seeing lately on consensus decision-making teams.

C-Suite Involvement Is High

Selling to the C-suite has been critical since the beginning of time; however, one of the most breakthrough trends that we have seen this decade is an increase in C-suite participation. Chorus, a conversation intelligence technology firm, has shown that C-suite participation on the buying side was up an average of 80% in 2020, and CFOs are 71% more common on sales calls now than tactical leaders.[51]

It appears that these numbers are still holding true: In March 2021, CxO participation on the buyer side was up 40%, 2021 over 2020.[52]

Interestingly, and we will come back to this in a few chapters, sales-side CxO participation increased dramatically as well in this period—more than 150%.[53]

These are the economic decision makers—the check-writers, the ones that control the budget. What is great about CxO involvement in the buying process is that they have the authority and ability to buy—one of our five essential Qualifying Characteristics. As a result, win rates increase by 38% when the C-suite is involved in the buying process. And here is something fascinating: C-suite stakeholders talk 8.5% more on deals that close. We think this is an important data point. When deals are won, the C-suite representatives are more engaged in meetings with salespeople. Our research also shows that deals that progress to the next buying stage include an average of five engaging questions asked by the rep to that C-suite stakeholder.

Five Characteristics of Qualified Prospects

1. *They have a need for what you sell and are aware of it.*
2. *They have both the authority and the ability to pay for it.*
3. *They have a relative sense of urgency about making a buying decision.*
4. *They have a significant level of trust in the salesperson and their organization.*
5. *They are willing to listen to the salesperson.*

What C-Level Folks Want Most

There is clearly a connection there. When the reps are asking engaging questions to CxO stakeholders, we can surmise that the salespeople are discussing the objectives and strategies of the business. And those are exactly the kind of conversations that will move sales forward. Let us look at the Decision Pyramid again; this time, we have filled in the typical rationales for each level of buyer in both the organizations we described earlier (traditional manufacturing, medical, and construction). Notice that the rationale for buying at the C-level is "strategic direction" or how the supplier can help the customer achieve larger goals than a single project, product, or transaction.

Figure 4: Rationale for Buying—Manufacturer

ROLE		RATIONALE FOR BUYING
CEO President Owner	**I**	Strategic Direction
Plant Manager Engineering Quality Manager	**II**	Implementation, Results
Operators Purchasing Agents	**III**	Maintain Status Quo, Minimize Change

There is a great story Russ tells a lot in training sessions. He was flying home from Denver, sitting in the window seat, and struck up a conversation with the fellow sitting in the aisle seat. It turned out that he was the retired CEO of a very large utility in Southern California, and he was returning from a board meeting in Denver. Russ explained that The Brooks Group did sales training, and the CEO said, "You know, we just had a board meeting, and our VP of Sales came in and said, 'I've instructed all of my sales team to immediately go call on the CEOs of all of our prospects and customers.' I cautioned the VP," he said:

> "Let me tell you my reality. When I was CEO and took a meeting with somebody, they had about three to five minutes to show me how they could help my company achieve its goals. You wouldn't believe how many people came in there and immediately started their normal customer product pitch. If that was the case, the meeting wrapped up pretty quickly, and they never got into my office—or even close to the executive floor—again as long as I was around.
>
> However, those who came in and could converse about my business—my strategy, the issues that I was facing and how they could help me overcome those? They were the ones who got to come back to continue the conversation. Those were the ones that I saw as adding value to my business."

Purchasing Departments: Friend or Foe?

According to the Procurement and Supply Australasia, "organizations with top-quartile procurement functions recovered from the global financial crisis of 2008 three years earlier on average relative to the companies with low-performing procurement functions."[54] It stands to reason that organizations that have highly functioning purchasing organizations will have been the fastest to react and adapt to the COVID era environment that has brought with it:

- Abundant supply chain issues
- Greater scrutiny on purchases due to tighter budgets
- Fear-based, risk-averse decision-making
- More people invested in the buying decision with more opinions and requirements

The key to working successfully with procurement is understanding the process they execute, their goals, and what they expect from a vendor relationship. Sales professionals must enter the buying process early, develop a deep understanding of an organization's purchasing process, and sell and negotiate with transparency in order to reach mutually satisfactory agreements.

Sellers, though, commonly regard procurement professionals as the adversary—there only to identify the lowest cost provider and squeeze profit margin even further. Many even hold to the false idea that procurement personnel personally profit from sharper negotiation or relationships with competitive vendors. But this procurement-as-the-enemy perspective has begun to change, especially for the most successful Hybrid Sellers. In recent years, the conventional stereotype of procurement professionals as "number-crunchers" has become less relevant as organizations begin to rely more heavily on them to create value rather than respond to cost pressures.

We mentioned this before, but it bears repeating: Research shows that price is no longer the sole driver of purchasing decisions. Our survey of 138 procurement professionals across a variety of industries—from manufacturing, OEM with distribution, and construction to government, healthcare, and technology services—revealed that only 7% of respondents cite price as their only consideration when making a purchasing decision. (It is certainly still a key factor, but it is often ranked below other things like on-time delivery, quality, responsive customer service, etc.)

What Do Procurement Professionals Want Most?

In order for sellers to create win-win solutions when dealing with procurement, they must fully understand the rules by which procurement professionals are operating, the systems in place to assist with making the buying decision, and the formal and informal roles procurement and purchasing professionals play in the decision process.

Let us take a look back at the Decision Pyramid.

In our business at The Brooks Group, we frequently start our conversations with the VP of Sales or the Head of

> *The key to working successfully with procurement is understanding the process they execute, their goals, and what they expect from a vendor relationship.*

Learning and Development. Yet we have learned to engage with purchasing soon after we have qualified the opportunity to understand any unique purchasing requirements the company may require, and to ensure they have reviewed our terms and conditions to remove any obstacles once we have agreed upon a program's definition.

What purchasing professionals want varies depending on what role they are playing in the decision-making process. At level one, they will be looking for capabilities in the company that align with purchasing priorities —onshoring, sustainability, transparency to the supply chain, etc. At level 3, they will be looking at the more historical price and delivery terms.

Structuring Your Sales Organization to Meet Your Customers Where They Want to Be Met

There is a useful phrase from golfing here: "You drive for show, and you putt for dough." Your existing customers will continue to be the ones that propel and keep your business strong. The most effective and resourceful companies have been rethinking the way they care for their customers in response to the changes a digitalized world has required of them. In the language of our analogy, they are working on their putting skills.

> *"Today's buyers have neither the time nor the desire to invest in a singular sales relationship with each of their suppliers. Over the course of the entire buy cycle they expect to interact with multiple team members and want the information they share throughout the process understood by all."* [55]

When your buyer needs an answer, they do not want to have to jump through hoops. They definitely do not want to hear, "Well, that's not my job...let me connect you with Francis in x department." Or worse, get a voice mail greeting that says how much they care about your call, and to leave a message that they will return later. From your buyer's perspective, you are one company, and they expect everyone they interact with to speak with one voice—24/7.

As a sales organization, you should think carefully about what practices, systems, and access points make the most sense for getting the customer the right solution or answer in the right way at the right time.

> *We worked with a company years ago that used a rep network. Every time sales managers met with the reps, the reps kept pleading for an app so that they could see accurate inventory status, get current pricing, and place orders, but management was struggling to find one that worked with the company's ERP system. It cost the reps business because they couldn't give their customers immediate answers to get an order off the street.*

> *In contrast, another of our customers changed the focus of their inside sales team from just supporting the outside salespeople to also being able to discuss needs with customers, take orders and deliver samples, and any other sales role. Rather than being threatened by this group, the outside salespeople saw how their customers responded to greater support and, as a result, the company has achieved a continuous number of years of record revenue.*

For example, here at The Brooks Group a few years back, we realized our own sales organization needed a little shakeup. Here is a snapshot of what changes we have implemented since then:

- We gave our senior salespeople support people who could handle straightforward customer conversations, as well as proposals and letter of agreement development.

- We also began bringing our subject matter experts—with emphasis on the kinds of research we can perform or had experience in various industries—into the selling conversation earlier to hear and understand what the real challenges are for our clients. That way, we can shape the training we offer to meet each specific client's expectations.

- Another helpful change we made was putting together some diagnostic tools to help us understand how aligned sales organizations are, so we can address the real key issues with which our customers are coming to us.

- From a sales process standpoint, we simplified our customer-facing documents, cleaning up our terms and conditions and our letters of agreement so that they are more complete, easier to read, and have all the information that customers need in one place.

- We also began looking deeper into deals in the end of our funnel (for us, that is the Apply, Convince, and Tie It Up stages) earlier in each month to see if a deal is really going to complete that month. If not, it immediately moves to the next month's forecast to give us a greater reliability in our forecasting.

- We created a major opportunities process that allows us to alert every person in the company, preparing us to move quickly to customize proposals, support meetings, or provide the appropriate reference from our hundreds of customers.

- Last, but definitely not least, and this is very important: We are also looking at how we can continue the selling conversation while our customer is going through their internal conversations by providing confidence-building information as they weigh a final decision.

One Company, One Voice

A 2016 LinkedIn report showed that lack of alignment between sales and marketing cost companies about 10% of potential revenue every year—a significant cost and burden on organizations. A 2020 study showed that 76% of customers expect consistent interactions across departments (marketing, sales, even customer service). Customers want a seamless experience and will vote with their pocketbooks, taking their business to the places where they will find that alignment. Fifty-four percent of them say that it feels like marketing, sales, and service are disconnected, proving a disjointed process. Looking at things from the customer's perspective—they do not see three different groups. They see one company. The internal challenge is to be one face, one voice, one message, and one reaction to the customer requests.

Think about your own sales organization. Is your buyer's experience with you seamless? If not, what can you do to adapt to the way your buyers want to have their account serviced?

Marketing + Sales In Tandem

As we all know, buyers are a little more reluctant, waiting longer to engage with sales; so what can sales and marketing do together in order to really bring those customers in and increase the quality of those conversations? LinkedIn commissioned a survey with Forrester in mid-2020 to look at how sales and marketing were working together.[56] The researchers acknowledged in this survey that sales and marketing together were going to be the big drivers of business recovery coping with the effects of the global pandemic.

They found B2B sales and marketing leaders say that sales and marketing alignment is largest opportunity for improving business performance today:

- Ninety-six percent of sales and marketing professionals see challenges with strategy alignment, due to different leadership, KPIs, and goals/objectives.

- Ninety-seven percent of sales and marketing professionals report issues with process alignment, due to different processes tools not being integrated.
- Ninety-seven percent of sales and marketing professionals face challenges with content and messaging alignment because the content is generated in silos and is product-focused instead of solution-focused.

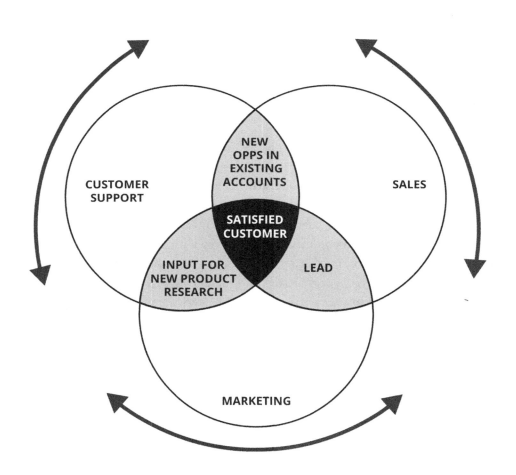

It is critical for business growth, especially in times when new prospects are hard to find. Ninety percent of sales and marketing professionals said that when your marketing initiatives and your messaging are aligned with sales, your customer experience is positively impacted. So, when your organization achieves better partnership and synchronicity between your marketing and sales initiatives, not only are you bringing more people and revenue in the door, but the customer's experience is better, and they are likely to stay with you.

Marketing and sales are both essential to any organization's survival. Depending on where one sits, though, it usually feels like one department is starved and the other department gets the lion's share of the budget. The biggest challenge is usually alignment, but that can also be related to timing. Salespeople are very driven to a month or quarter, and marketing can easily think longer term.

Fixing this misalignment of purpose and timing starts at the top. Most companies that put sales and marketing under one leader struggle because, even though it is a good idea in theory, whomever runs a sales and marketing organization is judged primarily on their sales numbers. Over time, less and less time is spent thinking about the marketing function, and more and more time gets spent thinking about the opportunities and end results, focusing on closing deals.

In contrast, companies that go the other route—having two leaders—makes sense structurally, but the challenge they face is that the two do not always effectively collaborate. If you are going to have a marketing lead and a sales lead, they must have well-defined roles in terms of not only who does what but how they are going to interact. Collaboration between the two must be built into the systems and structures of the organization.

Over the last five to ten years, we have seen companies implement the idea of a field marketing or product marketing organization that is more closely aligned with sales. The overall purpose of that organization is to address the question, "How do we drive leads and opportunities?" This can happen across all channels—telephone calls, email, print advertising, working inside existing customers, and so on—not just on the web.

Regardless of how your organization manages its sales and marketing efforts, the collaboration cannot only be at the top. There needs to be opportunities for sales and marketing teams to talk together, especially around the topic of lead generation. Together, they can assess who are the best customers—both in terms of who is buying your products today and potentially who you want to buy your products tomorrow. (Of course, there may be disagreement, so there needs to be work in terms of balance, and data should be your ultimate guide.) Our best advice for keeping marketing and sales aligned is to ensure marketing people are invited to—and expected to—sit in on weekly sales calls. What are people hearing? What are the issues that customers are having?

We would also recommend including marketing in any major deal strategy conversations. We have a client that has implemented these interdepartmental sessions weekly—salespeople bring their most leverageable opportunities to the table and brainstorm how to move them forward. This gives marketing insight into what prospects want/need for improved messaging, as well as additional support resources to support throughout the sales process.

When they are hearing directly from sales, marketing can meld what they hear with the data and insights they have collected to craft messages that really speak to the issues occurring in your marketplace. Once marketing has put the fishing lines out there, sales and marketing teams need to assess together to which messages your customers are best responding. Every week they can review the numbers being generated and do a deep dive into the conversion rates. Marketing

> *Customers want a seamless experience and will vote with their pocketbooks, taking their business to the places where they will find that alignment.*

can help answer the important question, "What is the most efficient and effective way to introduce ourselves and engage with companies?"

The Inside-Outside Sales Balance

In response to customer shifts, there has been significant blending and/or retooling of the traditional inside and outside sales roles. Where, historically, inside sales has been used to qualify leads to pass along to outside or field reps, nowadays, inside sales are allowed to close big deals on their own in many firms. We are finding that, in most companies, sales leaders need to redefine exactly what is the inside sales role and expand their vision of what inside salespeople can do.

Our clients, at least, are on board: In a recent survey we did, more than half of our folks are saying they are going to use more inside salespeople or more account retention people as they go forward in 2021 and beyond. We think Russ's old boss summed this up nicely years ago—he was ahead of his time—"Sales sells the first unit; everybody else in the company sells the second unit and every one after."

The SaaS industry is a leader in this movement. Many of our clients close six- or seven-figure agreements purely with inside salespeople. They have the ability to connect, discover, and recommend solutions and even perform demonstrations without ever setting foot inside the account. The outside salespeople, if they exist, are managing large geographic or vertical territories and see the inside team as equal members of engagements. When an on-site visit is required, the outside salespeople build the agenda and strategy for the meeting alongside the inside people, and even have them virtually participate.

Relationship Management

Speaking of account retention, companies may have account managers, retention specialists, customer service reps, technical implementation people, and other professionals whose job has historically been doing the work that keeps customers happy. While these jobs are no less important today—and, in fact, may be more important than ever—the way those departments interact with inside and outside sales needs to change if it has not already.

One of our clients in the fashion industry has two sales teams: One responsible for getting new suppliers to let them distribute products via their platform, and the second responsible for growing the supplier business over the long-term. Both groups were successful before we engaged with them, but what we discovered in our conversations was that frequently the original goals of the suppliers were not passed along to the second team, causing confusion and frustration on the part of the customer, and information having to be shared a second time with our client. This was remedied with more consistent use of the CRM, and short "handoff" meetings between the different salespeople on the teams.

Coordinating It All

Whatever the title, *someone* has ultimate responsibility for ensuring that the customer's experience lives up to what they were promised. Whether it is the salesperson or an account manager or someone else leading the initiative, they need to buy into the vision of team-based selling. Today's sales teams can collaborate in countless ways, allowing every member of the team to access up-to-the-minute data and information. In these new structures, there is a lot less hierarchy and a lot more communication. Technology tools empower every team member with knowledge, insight into current and long-term goals, and, most importantly, up-to-date results for a customer. A call can start with a congratulations on improvements seen or knowing that the salesperson is likely to be chastised for underperformance. Team selling empowered by the right technology is now enabling top-performing organizations to react with agility and resilience to just about any challenge or opportunity thrown at them.

Communication and Upskilling to Manage the Essential Handoffs

Where are the handoffs that are needed in your customers' interactions with your company? Are you set up for effective strategic account management?

At The Brooks Group, we have found that, for many of our clients, each customer's expectations lead to questions internally, such as, "Who is compensated for what?," and, sometimes, "Why is that my job?" Clarifying roles and responsibilities for all parts of the sales effort is essential, as is building pay plans that reward individual and team progress on KPIs. As a sales leader, you also should think carefully about who is right for each type of role. Once you have the right people in the right places, are expectations as clear for internal folks as they are for outside folks?

It is worth noting that installing any new system—whether it is software or a business procedure—takes training and buy-in from your team.

In the following chapters, we're going to delve into how Hybrid Sellers win deals in the face of aggressive cost competition, and explore the types of upskilling that are required for your sales team members.

Key Takeaways from This Chapter

- While we have more access to data than ever, the volatility we have been seeing in the world—across markets and industries—has challenged our forecasting ability. **If you cannot look ahead with confidence, you must be able to ensure that your organization can respond rapidly and assertively to variability and opportunities.**
- Your customers are showing their own agility by changing their buying processes to minimize risk and ensure purchases align with or advance larger strategic initiatives. **To thrive, your sales organization must adapt to these expectations, even if it means reorganizing your own structures to deliver a better customer experience and capture every opportunity.**
- **C-suite involvement in decision-making and consensus decision-making involving various stakeholders are de rigueur with today's complex and/or high-value B2B purchases.** Understanding the buying organization (see Contact Map and Decision Pyramid) will allow your salespeople to make recommendations that focus on what each individual wants and needs (and have many points of contact for information about changes in the business or marketplace).
- Customers want a seamless experience and will vote with their pocketbooks, taking their business to the places where they will find that alignment. **Team selling empowered by smart technology is imperative for organizations that understand the importance of being agile and resilient in responding to customer requirements and providing the type of sales interactions they desire.**

Ask Yourself

- How well are my salespeople entrenched in their accounts (or prospective accounts)? Do they know the key personnel and have an understanding of each person's possible buying motivations?

- What can I do to incentivize and systematize agility in my team?

- What reorganization (if any) do I need to consider to ensure my sales team can adapt to customer expectations and capture all relevant opportunities?

- What does "team selling" look like at my organization? Are we truly able to meet our customers and prospects at any point in their buying process with valuable guidance and support?

CHAPTER 6 FREE TOOL
Account Contact Mapping

https://brooksgroup.com/download-tools/

Chapter

7

Facing Down Aggressive Cost Competitors

In our Sales Leader Forums—weekly get-togethers with small groups of about eight peers who are sales leaders—we hear a lot of conversation about real-time challenges they are facing. Lately, we've heard concern centered around the following three problems:

1. Senior reps, who are challenged by digital selling tools and methods.
2. Questions about what kind of retraining is needed to get outside reps, who consider themselves to be in-person salespeople, comfortable selling without being physically present.
3. Pricing, which has always been a big issue in sales, and is now amplified in our present environment.

While the first two are clearly related to the effects of the pandemic and work-from-home, virtual meetings, and travel moratoriums, the third is a longstanding complaint from sales leaders and salespeople alike. The idea around value selling—or how to hold onto gross margin—is one of the most-requested topics by our clients at The Brooks Group. The dynamics of virtual negotiation have complicated the effectiveness of value selling, for sure, but learning new ways to approach the sale will help your salespeople capture and sell the value that your company and its products/services bring.

Price Pressure Is Real and Constant

In one nine-week study we did during 2020, we sought to understand the impact of price pressure on B2B organizations. In our survey, we asked whether the pressure to lower prices was an issue for our respondents:

- 75% said, "yes."
- 23% said, "no."
- 2% indicated that it is not applicable (likely they sell at a fixed price, so the pressure to change it just does not apply).

Then, we asked the same folks how much price pressure they have experienced in the last month:

- 23% indicated it's been a significant issue.
- 51% said it's been moderate.
- 21% reported NO price pressure.
- 6% said, "not applicable" (because they weren't then able to actively sell).

In terms of amount of price concessions, numbers varied widely, but all were between 5% and 15%. Some folks also said that they were seeing a trend of requests to extend payment terms: Instead of net 30, customers are asking for net 60, 90, or even 120 days.

Coming out of a survey run in October 2021, 32% of respondents indicated that their most important strategic sales priority was strengthening margins and profitability. (This response came in second only to winning new accounts—a priority for 36% of our respondents.)

As a follow-up, we asked what three challenges would limit their team's ability to achieve their strategic sales priority. Supply chain issues was the number one challenge for 67% of our respondents, 63% indicated that economic conditions impacting customers would be a challenge, and 48% noted that economic conditions impacting their own organizations would be a limiting factor. The last two likely are a function of pricing.

We have already mentioned that buyer discount requests increased in 2020. In our October 2021 survey, 52% of respondents indicated no change in customer discount requests from 2020. However, 48% noted that customer discount requests or negotiation attempts had, in fact, increased.

These data suggest that price pressure will continue, if not increase, in the 2020s—driven by the need for sales organizations to increase prices due to product availability (or lack thereof) and the economic squeeze felt by many B2B buyers.

"Please Share Our Pain"

The variety of reasons buyers report for asking for price concessions is interesting:

- Some are asking because of their own need to cut costs—they see that their business is down, and they need some help from suppliers to achieve profitability targets.
- Sometimes they are asking because they recognize that you, as a provider, are facing decreased demand—so, therefore, you may be a little hungrier to make the sale.
- Some may be asking because of their need to manage costs against their own competitors—they may be looking to you to share the burden of increased raw material costs.

One of the things we heard that really made sense was a salesperson who described it this way: "Our customers are saying, 'Please share our pain: If we're going to take a hit, we need you to take a hit as well.'"

That said, frequently the reason your sales team faces pricing pressure is that buyers are trained to push back—that is especially true for purchasing and procurement professionals. For some, it can be almost like a game in which they are just trying to see how much they can get you to give up. The harsh reality, though, is that often it is the salespeople who have trained buyers of all types to ask for price concessions.

One of Russ's stories involves a sales ride-along a few years ago. The salesperson he accompanied had a unique product with significant advantages over the customer's current supplier. The salesperson presented a quotation for the units. As the customer read through the

quote, without even waiting for a comment, the salesperson blurted out,
"We can do better on the pricing." Not only did the comments impact the
trustworthiness of the salesperson, it communicated that whatever price
I offer you next is likely negotiable as well. Plus, he forgot the strength of
the value he offered.

Ultimately, if you are not hitting your margins and your salespeople are constantly facing price pressure, there is one reason. They are not selling value. Only when you are selling based on what your prospects and customers value can you overcome price hesitancy or challenges.

Collaboration Is the Key

Collaboration is really the key to successfully negotiating a deal that keeps your profit margin, while satisfying your new customer and making them feel that they are getting good value for their investment. Sure, the term *collaboration* is so over-used, it almost does not mean anything (kind of like "we want to partner with you," right?). But, really, if sales does its job in following along with the buyer's journey, you're collaborating throughout.

Collaboration starts with not rushing through the sale. Take the time to learn what the person values (which means the right preparation for the call and good probe questions). Do not just email in the quote, but also discuss your fit to their needs and wants and get agreement that you have a solution before presenting price. Walk the customer through the price in the context of the value you are bringing. These meetings/discussions take time and collaboration—talking with, not talking at, a customer. This is nowhere truer than in negotiation. Sales *must* have the buyer's active involvement in the process.

You cannot win a negotiation on your first response, but you can sure lose it. Instead of launching into a defense of your position—or worse, agreeing to take the offered terms—try responding with a question like, "Why do you feel that way?" or even, "How am I supposed to do that?" when the buyer asks for a price decrease. Negotiation, like selling, must start with understanding.

A study done by Neil Rackham and a team of researchers looked at what expert negotiators do differently. Among their findings (as reported in Adam Grant's Think Again) was, when compared to average negotiators, skilled negotiators are more likely to focus on common ground (38% to 11%) and ask more questions (21.3% to 9.6%).[57]

Expert negotiators recognize what we have been discussing—that **value comes from the grouping of attributes in an offer** rather than just price. For example, right now, the big thing we are seeing from working with clients is that they're looking for supply chain assurance. Common questions we hear include, "Am I really going to get what I want, especially if some things are being manufactured overseas?" and "Can you help me protect my inventory?" and "Seeing these wild swings, is now a good time to discuss concepts such as vendor-managed inventory?" or "Given the load on my people, is there a way you can help with training and/or deployment?"

Recognize that buyers ultimately will be asked by their manager if they negotiated a "good deal," so help them be able to communicate how they received good value by sharing the points where your offering makes sense beyond just the price. The sale is not complete until the buyer sees and can communicate your value.

When Negotiation Does Not Work

If you are reading this book, you are likely a curious sales leader who is always looking for ways to improve the way your sales team goes about its business. You know that following a selling system—any selling system (of course, we are partial to IMPACT Selling)—greatly improves the likelihood of a successful sale. Up to this point in this book, we have written a lot about changes in the world of professional selling and focused intently on the

> *Negotiation, like selling, must start with understanding.*

concept that the buyer's journey through a buying process can be mapped out. We hope that we have convinced you that if sales professionals mold their sales process to where in the buying process their prospects and customers are, they will have far more success, in terms of meeting with the right people, discovering what is truly valued by the customer, and especially be able to communicate the superiority of their solution over competitive offerings for that opportunity.

But, as a sales leader, you also know that winning the sale at any cost is not good business. You know that maintaining profit margins on your products and services is essential to staying in business. So where does it all go wrong?

To state it plainly, most people are bad negotiators. Something like 80% of CEOs and managers, when tested, leave money on the table in contract negotiations. And those are some of the folks who should have the most vested interest in maintaining margin. That is not even research about folks who are selling widgets day in and day out as salespeople. In our own recent surveys, we are noticing some trends—some good and some terrible.

First, the best:

- Some folks are standing their ground on discounts and removing items or features or reconfiguring their proposals rather than losing margin.

Then, the good:

- Some are coming out with lower cost product lines or services.

Then, the terrible (which is the majority, unfortunately):

- They are "splitting the difference."
- They are just giving the discount that is requested.

We all know that every dollar percentage point we give up in the deal immediately reduces the bottom line. That is an unacceptable outcome, especially if your desire is to deliver a truly superior product and/or service, to be able to invest in new and innovative offerings, or if you or your team are compensated based on margin.

Behind most cost-cutting lie three poor thought processes based on seemingly logical points. Let us look at each and dissect it a bit.

#1: I Will Make It Up in Volume.

It does not matter how many times this has been written about, practiced optimistically, and even joked about (*since 1833*[58]). Salespeople who consider themselves true professionals still make the mistake of thinking that they can make up in volume what they lose in margin. It even sounds plausible. Unfortunately, the simple fact is that the math just does not work. If you are losing margin or money on the price of a single item that you sell, you are losing margin or money on every unit. You could sell millions of units, and you would still be losing.

#2: The Fixed Pie

The Fixed Pie Perception is the construct—the misperception—that you believe that the buyer's interests and priorities are in direct opposition to your own interests and priorities as a sales professional. If I am trying to make a sale with a high margin, the buyer *must* be focused on getting me to lower my price.

However, survey after survey says the most critical issue for companies is not price. It is things such as supply, quality, the reputation of the company that is providing them, and so on. These items all have value that should be reflected in whatever price you charge. Most are also negotiable, so bringing greater value in one of these areas supports the price you are charging, even when it is higher than a competitive offering. Working together, a salesperson and a buyer can expand the options reviewed and the price associated with the complete package of value. Salespeople cannot just assume that they are in an adversarial relationship with prospects.

#3: You Can Just Split the Difference

There is a big problem with the "split the difference" approach or, as Northwestern University and others over the years have called it, *satisficing*. In this situation, you become convinced you are racing to an agreement, because decision-makers frequently select the first option that meets their needs and wants, or they choose the one that seems to address the most needs—but in neither case are they choosing the true "optimal" solution.

Think about it. Your company has set a standard price for your product or service based on a number of factors—cost of supply, overhead costs, profit, etc. When a customer's buyer offers you a price—say, 70% of your standard price—their logic is often purely, "I want it for less." When you are racing to a solution and say "let's split the difference" at, say, 85% of your standard price, you have given away rationalized value for a random discount ask. It seems like a fast solution, but, in reality, you have been played. They likely wanted a 15% discount all along and could read your eagerness to get what they wanted.

Some of you may know about a negotiation exercise called *The Batmobile*. In the exercise, two people come together around a used car: one is selling, and one is buying. The car has a scrap value of a certain amount. It turns out that if you are the seller and you move quickly to make a decision, you usually end up with a suboptimal deal. Why? Because you are contrasting the scrap value of the car with whatever is slightly greater than that number.

Yet in the brilliance of the exercise, the truth is that the buyer is really looking just to purchase the door as a replacement for another vehicle they own. Since the scrap value of the automobile is exactly the same whether it has a door or does not have a door, taking the time to understand the buyer's true need significantly increases the value received by the seller. Done right, the buyer gets a door for less than the scrap value of the vehicle, and the seller gets that amount plus scrap value. A true win-win, expanded pie solution.

We are quite certain that at least some of your salespeople buy into at least one of the fallacies we just described—they are very common. Their success at negotiating and hanging onto margin is directly tied to the relationship dynamics they set up with their prospects, their attitude about the value of the products/services they sell, and the skills they bring to bear at the negotiating table.

Sales leaders, please hear us. It is your job (and we are aware that sometimes it is quite challenging) to work with your sales team to change mindsets. In his classes, Russ likes to remind people, "Of course the buyer asks for a lower price, that's their job. But remember, your job is to get the pricing your company requests." This discussion is not superfluous to selling, it is a key component of a successful sale.

Many salespeople want to maintain the relationship at all costs, especially since up to this point the selling process has been about building a good working relationship. But they are working against achieving their own selling goal. Why? Good purchasing people are trained in negotiation and use this behavioral attribute against the seller. The ironic result is usually not a better relationship, but one where the purchaser feels advantage can be taken of the seller. As a sales leader, it is important for you to understand how each individual on your selling team approaches negotiations. This is critical coaching information.

How to Get to Optimal Solutions

It takes time to get to the point where the seller and the buyer are on the same page about what is the optimal solution. The only real way to get there is by capturing—and communicating—value from the very beginning of the sales cycle. If buyers don't trust your company's sellers, they are not going to share real, truthful information about what they value.

One of our founder Bill Brooks' oft-quoted "Sales Truths" is:

> *All sales degenerate into a struggle over price in the absence of a value interpreter. If your sales team are constantly being pressured by prospects and customers to drop their prices, they're not seeing enough value in your company's products or services to offset the price your salespeople are asking them to invest.*

Because the buyer's process has changed so much in recent years, we, as sales professionals, must use our sales skills in a different way. In training, we use the analogy that salespeople are like woodworkers who have been doing framing construction but now must switch to doing finish carpentry. Most of the tools in the toolbox are the same, but we must use them differently.

The most important thing sales professionals must believe is that most problems are not solved by price; and, in fact, sometimes dropping your price can have a negative impact on buyers' perception of you, your products/services, and your organization. Plus, it may cost you *and* your customers more in the long run.

For example, let us say you are in lighting supplies, and you are working with a contractor who is pushing you to drop your price based on a competitor's offer. What happens if they cannot get delivery, or it comes in the wrong size? What is the cost to the contractor at that point? If one of their crews is sitting idle for a day due to lack of components, what does it cost them? When there is a problem, the contractor has to go back to the business owner or the homeowner to fix the problem, which also costs something. So, make sure you are capturing all that value in the offering you are bidding—availability, fit, shipping, warranty, quality, and price.

Will the buyer automatically recognize these? Maybe. Will they communicate them to the seller? Rarely. It is the job of the salesperson to be the "value interpreter" when selling.

The Value Formula (Again)

We keep referring to value, which is a pretty abstract idea, as if it is something you can hold in your hand. In Chapter 2, we presented the definition of Value as "Perceived Benefits divided by Perceived Price and/ or Perceived Emotional Cost." We did not get too deeply into it, so let us remedy that now.

Here is how it works. If your prospects believe that the benefits that they will receive by purchasing your product or service are greater than what they will pay for it (price), plus any difficulties with terms, conditions, transition, implementation, retraining, spare parts, etc. (perceived emotional cost), your prospect sees value. If this occurs, you will have minimal problem with price.

However, if the opposite is perceived, you will face problems. If the prospect feels that the benefits they will receive from your product or service are not sufficient to justify the price and perceived emotional cost, they will either (a) not make a purchase, or (b) push back on your price.

What is cool is that you can take the Value Formula and turn it into a nice visual representation of what your value proposition is for each niche into which you sell. Here is an example:

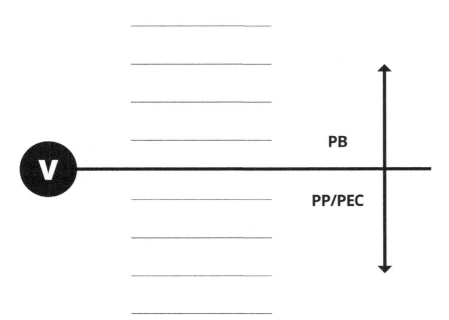

Remember our specialty building materials distributor client? As part of our discovery work, their stakeholders asked us to identify their value proposition. We asked sales team members why customers do business with them, and they overwhelmingly cited their "relationships" with customers, as well as their service and product quality. We then asked a few key clients (representing their "ideal accounts") what was most important to them in choosing a vendor. We sought to further define terms like *relationships*, *service*, and *quality* to truly understand where the company can differentiate. For them, order accuracy price, on-time performance, seller accessibility, and product availability were most important.

What is Most Important?

CUSTOMERS

1. **Order Accuracy**
2. **Price**
3. **On-Time Performance**
4. **Accessibility**
5. **Product Availability**

MANAGERS

1. **Order Accuracy**
2. **On-Time Performance**
3. Product Availability
4. Responsiveness
5. Expertise of Team

SUPPLIERS

1. Visibility
2. **On-Time Performance**
3. Product Availability
4. **Order Accuracy**

This misalignment of where each group saw value delivered meant that salespeople and customers were not optimizing pricing outcomes. If you do not know what a buyer really wants from you and how they view your offering, you will have miscommunication. Salespeople must be value interpreters, mapping what their organization offers with the needs and wants of the customers. Too many salespeople leave this "interpretation" to the customer, so value is lost. It is a perfect analog to a discussion with someone who speaks a foreign language you do not understand. Without an interpreter, you will both move to the lowest common denominator—

usually hand signals. With interpretation, value nuance is highlighted and used to justify your full price.

The value formula enables an effective salesperson to visually map the reasons to complete and not complete the sale from the customer's perspective and provides talking points to emphasize (perceived benefits) and potential areas to resolve (perceived emotional costs) with special offerings—for example, offering training to remove a customer's fear of change.

Building Value-Based Solutions

Sometimes the value is obvious to customers. Sometimes it is not. If your initial price is higher than a competitor, for example, but your expected product life is much longer, your transaction may add to unit price, but reduce overall warranty costs for the organization. Russ recently worked with a global chemical supplier whose products added a few cents to each product manufactured, but enabled significantly lower production line stoppages for maintenance. The result was a few cents per unit translated into more than six times that amount in greater production volumes and reduced labor costs for second-shift operations.

To be successful, the salesperson for the account had to get someone in management to recognize and endorse the change as an overall money saver for the company. If the salesperson had only worked with purchasing, the focus would have been per-unit pricing, with the likely result being reduced product pricing for our client.

Three Ways to Fix Price Dropping on Your Sales Team

If your sales team seems to be just indiscriminately dropping prices, you definitely have got a training issue. In the following sections, we will take a quick look at how we typically advise sales leaders with a price-dropping problem on their team.

#1. In the Short Term: Value Analysis

Use the Value Formula tool for your team to gain a clear value analysis of *this* transaction for *this* customer. It will illustrate why they, not a generic customer, should buy from you, specifically (Perceived Benefits), and also why they might have reservations (Perceived Price/Perceived Emotional Costs) about it. Remember that *perceived* is a key word, because all value is determined in the eye of the beholder. So, for one transaction a price might be perceived as "high," where in another the same price might be perceived as "low." Every member of your sales team needs to understand how strong your value case is on a deal-by-deal basis and be able to articulate it clearly in terms the prospect or customer will understand in the recommendation.

You can use the Value Formula as a checkpoint for every potential deal. Here is an example of how it might work in coaching. Let us say a sales professional is lobbying to give a discount to one of their customers.

> *The sales manager says to the rep, "I need to understand your value case. What are we bringing to this deal that could ensure we'll win, and why won't the customer buy from us?"*
>
> *The salesperson's answer is something like, "Well, we don't really know. It's a toss-up."*
>
> *Once she is peeled off the ceiling, the sales manager then would respond, "I'm not sure you've really discovered the true value of our solutions for this prospect. You need to go back and do a little more work in the account to understand what's really important."*

#2. Compensation Plan "Fixes"

Realigning compensation plans around net margin is an excellent way to refocus your salespeople on holding firm on price. When they are asked to cut price, they will end up sharing some of the loss.

One of our clients went from compensating reps on overall created revenue to a more complex formula of generated gross margin dollars. What they discovered was not only a two or three percent increase in margin points, but salespeople spent less time on low- or no-profit deals.

#3. Deal Desk

In our experience, we have seen that in every sales organization, there are certain reps who like to give up price more than others. One of the things we suggest to help course-correct this situation is to create a Deal Desk, where every deal above a certain revenue amount or that falls below a specific margin threshold is reviewed by a cross-functional team that has the authority to make decisions about all aspects of a deal. They can move allocations up or down, they can make decisions about pricing, they can look at whether you include or do not include free freight, and so on. They are looking across the business at a set of KPIs in terms of what they are winning: What's the deal size? When and where can we upsell?

One company we know implemented a Deal Desk in a very competitive marketplace. What they discovered nearly immediately was every participating department got a better sense of how they could contribute to a sale, how difficult it is to forecast, and the pain of being out of stock on certain items. At the same time, win percentages increased, because salespeople dug deeper to understand what was really valued and were able, through the Deal Desk, to make better trade-offs for company profitability.

The goal of the Deal Desk is not to slow down the transaction. Salespeople should bring a prepared deal and be able to get approval in one meeting, to be denied, or to look at enhancements in one quick call. It makes sure that if you are offering special terms in one part of the business it is an option for all similar customers, driving consistency and discipline in your in your pricing. According to research done by PwC, Deal Desks help you do a better job of capturing value.[59] In their review of historical data, they found Deal Desks:

- Reduce your sales cycle by anywhere from 25% to 40%
- Enhance your sales productivity by 15% to 20%
- Create a 5%–10% higher average sales price and invoice amount

Our experience here at the Brooks Group has shown similar successes.

So, getting everybody there who can make the decision—especially if your supply is constrained—is very important. Another great reason to implement a Deal Desk is it also provides real-time market data that are not just useful to the sales and marketing team. If you have always wanted to be able to share with those other departments what is really happening in the field, this is a good way to do it.

These Boots Are Not Made for Walking

Prioritization. Focus. Optimization. All are great words, but words that clearly imply that some accounts or opportunities will not be great, and possibly not even good. In fact, we would wager that as you think through what you have learned in this chapter, you will find that some "opportunities" in your pipeline or in your order book will rank as poor—yep, business you would never take today if you knew what you know now.

What are your salespeople to do? All of their training and instincts say, "Keep pressing and win the business," or, "My company will figure out a way to make it more profitable somehow." But the reality is some accounts will always be bad business. They are not profitable, or they are not as profitable as your targets for business should be. (In our experience, they also tend to be more demanding and slower paying.)

We started this book by saying sometimes your company gets fired. It is equally true that sometimes, you need to fire a customer.

In the first class he taught for The Brooks Group, Russ was asked about a specific account one of the salespeople in attendance was struggling with:

> *"I've been working with this account for about a year," reported the salesperson. "And we can't find a solution. He needs two connectors and a ribbon cable. Our best price is $3.25, and the maximum amount he can pay is $2.75. What can I do?" After confirming the two numbers and asking a few other questions, my response was to walk away. "Walk away?" exclaimed the salesperson, "I can't walk away. I have a year invested in this account!"*

The reality of the situation was easy to see. If the best price the salesperson could offer as a vendor was $3.25, and the prospect only could pay $2.75, there was no way the business could be done at a profitable level. Unfortunately, most situations are not that straightforward.

When do you know you need to walk away? When the cost of the account is higher than the reward from the account.

What do we count in the cost? Everything from gross margin, cost of support, and cost of product changes or special requests to any cost associated with change orders or other variants to your normal process.

When working with our clients, sometimes we will ask them to rank customers by gross margin, or total revenue and gross margin. This helps them analyze which—if any—accounts are ones with which to discuss a price increase or make a tough decision to walk away. Ultimately, companies are in business to make money, and if all you are doing is passing the same amount of money from your suppliers through your accounts receivable from your customer, it is time to walk away.

The second time that it might make sense to walk away from an account is if your market focus changes. If you have been serving a certain vertical or geographic market and you have decided to leave that market, you should look at continued cost to serve existing account(s). Usually, it makes sense to continue to supply them for a while until the product ages out (or is replaced by a new one) or cost of service grows too large.

Ultimately, you do not want the focus of this to be walking away from accounts, but, rather, freeing up limited sales time to focus on better accounts—larger, more profitable, etc. It is a bit like terminating an underperforming employee, which can be emotionally difficult, but everyone who works with them will be relieved.

Please, Sir, May I Have Some More?

For most salespeople, asking for a price increase from an existing customer can seem akin to getting a root canal. Research from Corporate Visions in 2021 shows that 69% of salespeople describe their price increase conversations as 50/50 or worse, with 55% of those salespeople stating they do not feel confident delivering the price increase message.[60] After working to win the business, then diligently servicing the account, a return visit to increase pricing—either due to rising costs from your suppliers or lower-than-contracted-volume purchases from the customer—can be challenging. But it is a task salespeople must undertake. Here is our advice on how to make the conversation more positive.

As preparation for the discussion about increasing prices, your salespeople should do their homework to understand what else is happening in the market with competitive pricing, what (if any) alternatives are available to their customer, and ensure they are confident in the justification for the price increase.

Remember: You cannot sell a product if you do not see the value of it yourself.

The most important aspect of a price increase discussion is for your salespeople to ensure they are reinforcing the "status quo." That is, they must explain the benefits that the customer has been receiving from working with your company, describe the degree to which you have created value together, and reaffirm the decision the customer made in selecting your company.

Once the value has been communicated, it is in that context that salespeople will raise the need to increase prices. Like presenting any price, they should be firm and confident in stating the new pricing and, if possible, explain clearly why your company has decided to take this action. (The price increase should not sound like it is a trial balloon and, therefore, open to negotiation.) One thing we practice with our client salespeople in training sessions is communicating pricing as clearly as they would answer the question, "What time is it?" We have them practice looking one another in the eye, first to answer, "What time is it?" and then, "What's the price going to be?" Both answers should be statements of fact, not the opening points in a debate.

Of course, salespeople should be prepared for objections: No customer "likes" a price increase. The most important factor in managing objections is not to let emotion color your response. When a buyer raises a concern, respond with a question, potentially related to the ones driving you to raise prices. For example, if you say that "Due to an increase in raw material costs, we are having to change the price to $x," and the customer objects, you could ask, "What are you experiencing with your own material suppliers?" or, "Help me understand your response—what are you seeing across the other products you buy?" As we write this in late 2021, supply chain issues are affecting most industries, so buyers are expecting price adjustments.

From this point forward, it becomes a discussion and should follow your normal process for objection handling. Realize that objection handling is mostly about skills: asking questions, seeking to learn more from the buyer, and seeing what options might be available to them. There are almost always options that make price increases more palatable; for example, things like placing orders before the effective date of the price increase, changing to a different product in your portfolio, and even discussing value engineering to a better solution (if possible).

Many salespeople want to maintain the relationship at all costs, especially since up to this point the selling process has been about building a good working relationship. But they are working against achieving their own selling goal. Why? Good purchasing people are trained in negotiation and use this behavioral attribute against the seller. The ironic result is usually not a better relationship, but one where the purchaser feels the seller can be taken advantage of. As a sales leader, it's important for you to understand how each individual on your selling team approaches negotiations. This is critical coaching information.

It is not at all uncommon for buyers to threaten "bringing in another supplier," but if you have communicated your value and understand the state of your industry, this may be a hollow threat. Stay engaged with the buyer, working through the price increase data until they accept it and have a plan for future orders.

It is not an easy conversation, but as Colin Powell said, "*There are no secrets to success. It is the result of preparation, hard work, and learning from failure.*"

> **Remember: You cannot sell a product if you do not see the value of it yourself.**

Key Takeaways from This Chapter

- Price pressure will continue, if not increase, in the 2020s—driven by the need for sales organizations to increase prices due to product availability (or lack thereof) and the economic squeeze felt by many B2B buyers.

- There are three cost-cutting fallacies that many salespeople mistakenly believe:

  1. You can make it up in volume.
  2. All buyers are exclusively focused on getting a lower price (The Fixed Pie).
  3. You can just split the difference.

- If your sales team is constantly being pressured by prospects and customers to drop their prices, they are not seeing enough value in your company's products or services to offset the price your salespeople are asking them to invest.
- The Value Formula:

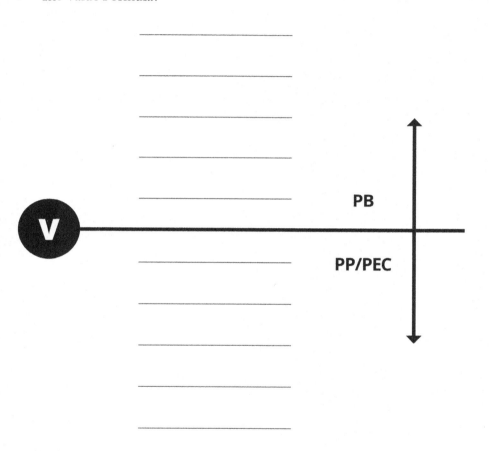

- There are three great ways to re-focus your salespeople if they are consistently cutting price:

1. Train them on the Value Formula and use it to assess every potential deal.
2. Realign your sales compensation plan around net margin.
3. Create a Deal Desk for potential deals over a certain size and/or complexity.

Ask Yourself

- Can my salespeople—in fact, can *I*—describe the Value Formula for our monthly "must close" opportunities?
- What does our compensation plan encourage now, if not margin? How could it be re-structured to encourage my salespeople to hold firm on price?
- If I were to implement a Deal Desk, who would need to be involved? What criteria would deals need to meet in order to be pursued?
- How do I feel about advising a salesperson to walk away from an opportunity when there is no way to differentiate so they can focus on more profitable business?

CHAPTER 7 FREE TOOL
Three Steps Toward a Collaborative Negotiation Tool
& Objections Worksheet

https://brooksgroup.com/download-tools/

Chapter
8

Today's Top Selling Strategy— Personalization

Having a consistent selling system combined with learnable personal and selling skills can make a salesperson effective in this new world of selling— even if buyers are doing more research on their own, inviting sales to the process later in the buying process, including more people on the buying team, and wanting to do more and more of the purchase decision through self-service means.

Sales is no longer a telephone book and a sample case. It requires strategies to target wider areas across a prospect's organization, and the skills to appropriately engage. This is a key reason why companies are increasingly expanding from product training to key selling skills, developing Hybrid Sellers equipped for success.

It seems that every new trend is built upon the failure or success of one before it. As we have described already, in this decade, the transition is occurring from "thought leadership," where vendors are encouraged to develop and share a never-ending amount of material on the solutions a prospect may be considering, to the salesperson being more of a guide through the material. Sellers are not only helping the prospect to determine what the important points to consider are for their organization, but also what the right ways are to weight the answers to these points. Not surprisingly, salespeople must be experts at understanding the unique, specific opportunities and challenges for each of their prospects' and customers' organizations—and they are all different.

In a Forrester Consulting study, the firm reported that four out of five buyers say they value sales content and interactions that are tailored to their business, industry, job/role, and the issues they must address. Sixty percent of customers will stop doing business with sellers that do not tailor solutions to meet their exact needs, and 43% of buyers feel embarrassed in front of their peers if sellers' presentations are not customized to their specific needs.[61]

The skill of guiding buyers through their buying journey—when information and even decision rubrics are unique for each customer—is a critical skill that can and must be learned.

But what, exactly, does a personalized sales interaction look like? It goes far beyond adding the prospect's name or logo on presentation materials, though that is a good start. A HubSpot study describes customer service experiences this way:

> *"Every interaction needs to revolve around the concept of individual value, mutual respect, and a shared vision for your future together as their brand of choice. Consider how you can let your customers know that:*
>
> • *They are more than a transaction to your organization.*
> • *Their time and money allow you to continue to pursue your mission.*
> • *Their journey as a person is a part of your journey as a business."* [62]

There are multiple factors that go into creating this type of relationship with buyers, beginning before the seller ever makes initial contact with anyone within the prospective customer's organization.

Personalizing sales interactions requires that salespeople engage fully in everything from creating a comprehensive plan for going after a new account and throughout the process of managing and growing profitable accounts:

• Assessing your accounts carefully to determine where you have the most likelihood of profitability, growth, or other positive factors.
• Developing a deep understanding of the unique corporate factors—strategies, goals, initiatives, etc.—that are at play within each strategically important account.
• Mapping the influences on each buying decision and understanding individuals' buying motivations.

- Articulating the value proposition that you, your company, and your products/services offer each specific prospect or customer—in the language they use and will find compelling.
- Communicating with individuals within prospect and customer organizations in the way that is most effective for each, based on your knowledge of company and individual goals and initiatives.

In this chapter, we are going to show you a few essential tools that will help your salespeople make the deep dive into their strategic accounts, uncovering the information they need to be able to guide their prospects and customers through the buying process.

Strong SAM Leads to Excellent Personalization

Strategic account management (SAM) is the process of gaining, growing, and retaining accounts that are significant to your organization. When you implement a clear, organized account management program, it enables your salespeople to build strong value-driven, long-term relationships with customers based on what makes each customer unique. It's also a key competency in orchestrating the resources needed to win competitive accounts requiring mid- and long-term sales efforts.

Not All Accounts Are Created Equal

Notice that we wrote "accounts that are significant to your organization." Not all accounts are created equal, and not every account is worth the same investment of your time and other resources. In our workshops, we often encourage salespeople to look at their accounts in terms of two criteria in order to determine how significant each is: payoff and positioning. Your higher priority accounts will have high growth potential, a high perception of your value, a reasonable level of account maintenance required, and a close alignment with your business purpose.

Payoff

What makes an account attractive for you?

- **Growth Potential**—Is there opportunity for growth within the accounts or can the account be leveraged to grow other accounts through referrals, value of the logo, etc.?
- **Profitability**—What is the actual profitability of your existing accounts or the potential profitability of your target accounts?
- **Perception of Your Value**—How do your accounts perceive the value you offer? (As we have discussed, the higher the perception of value, the less price sensitive these accounts will be.)
- **Degree of Account Maintenance**—How much time must you spend with these accounts in relation to the amount of business you do with them? Are they high-touch with low reward?
- **Alignment with Your Business Offerings and Philosophy**—Are the accounts a good fit for your solutions and how they do business?

Payoff & Positioning Matrix

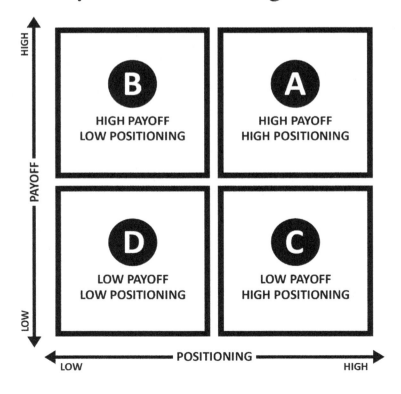

Positioning

How do your accounts personally view your salesperson, your organization, and your offerings compared to the competition? A favorable rating in any or all of these areas pushes the account toward the "high" side of the spectrum versus the "low." Sales leaders know that knowledge and consistency are key to maintaining and growing accounts.

---

5 Strategies for Successful Account Management

1. ***Probe key contacts to determine their receptivity toward discussing future directions for their organization.*** *If they are receptive, do it. If they are not, work on your relationship until they are. How can you improve your relationship?*

2. ***If your key contacts do not have access to strategic plans, work with them to identify and make contact with the person or people who do.*** *How do you do this?*

3. ***Provide highly valuable, insightful information for your key contacts every time you meet.*** *Reciprocity will then make them want to do the same. Like what?*

4. ***Create a picture of what you can do to help the customer's organization*** *so that they readily see how you can help other essential stakeholders in the organization. How can you do this?*

5. ***Work hard to be the single best supplier you can be.*** *Be 110% dependable and earn the right to achieve preferred vendor/supplier status. Make your key contacts look good. How can you do this?*

Understanding What Is Unique Within Each Account

Once your salespeople are confident about *which* of their accounts are deserving of the most investment of time and effort, they'll need to take things a step further in exploring the details about each account that make it unique.

If you recall the Decision Pyramid, the bottom two levels are most focused on tactical issues such as implementation, getting short-term results, maintaining the status quo, and minimizing change. As a result, if sales is engaged in conversations only on the bottom two levels, it will seriously limit opportunities for your organization—people in these roles tend to focus only on one initiative or outcome at a time.

No matter which functional area(s) of an organization—finance, purchasing, engineering, IT, etc.—with which you are engaged, sales will uncover a broader range of opportunities the further up the pyramid the salesperson can move the conversation. (We will spend some time later in this chapter looking at C-suite and procurement functions.)

Individuals playing the key roles in your prospects' and customers' organizations—the CxOs and decision makers—all are responsible for guiding their companies' strategies and setting the goals that allow their team to get results. Pay attention to the strategic view that informs each buyer's journey. Each individual will have different underlying:

- **Goals.** A business typically has a small number of strategic goals that drive all of their actions. These goals typically remain the same over time unless the business changes its strategy.
- **Objectives.** Using the goals as a starting point, the business will set objectives—action-oriented milestones that it sets out to accomplish within a defined time frame. (These are often revisited annually.)
- **Challenges.** Each business faces challenges in achieving its objectives, whether they are internal, market-driven, competitive, or other challenges. Surfacing these challenges in your discussions with your stakeholders will help you to better understand opportunities to support the stakeholder and to shape solutions that specifically target challenges.
- **Initiatives.** From a business's objectives, it defines initiatives: specific projects it will undertake to achieve the objectives. A business will frequently have more than one initiative underway at any given time.
- **Outcomes.** These are the results by which the business measures the success of its initiatives.

We recently worked with a software company that licenses complex modeling software to public agencies and private companies. When dealing with individuals at layers 2 and 3 of the decision maker pyramid, they found themselves discussing only a small portion of what the software was truly capable of doing. The software includes five

significant areas of modeling capability, and most purchasers only used one.

After training, as they started having more conversations with individuals at level 1, the conversations became more about how multiple portions of the software could help the agencies solve new problems, or the private companies grow their services into previously unaddressed areas of the business. Our client is transitioning from vendor to partner for these groups.

Growth (the organizational objective) was meeting an obstacle defined as lack of capability (obstacle). Working together, our client and their customers launched new initiatives that are starting to show positive outcomes. Our client reports that had they not had higher-level conversations, it is unlikely the initiatives would have been started, because too many people were unaware of the capabilities the organization already possessed.

Here is an example from our own sales team here at The Brooks Group. If sellers understand a customer's big picture strategy, and the objectives, obstacles, and initiatives associated with it, they may open more opportunities for their offerings. Conversely, if they only inquire about a specific initiative, they may get one piece of the solution but miss a bigger application. For example:

- A customer's GOAL may be to double revenue in five years.
- One of their OBJECTIVES may be to increase sales by 20%; perhaps another objective may be to reduce operating expenses by 8%.
- An OBSTACLE to increasing sales by 20% may be that the sellers do not have the right selling skills; another OBSTACLE may be that there is too much turnover on the sales team, so the team is not functioning at full capacity.
- One INITIATIVE to address the obstacle and accomplish the objective may be to implement sales training; but another INITIATIVE may be to revamp their sales hiring process.

If one of our sellers only probes about the sales training opportunity but does not ask about the bigger strategy, they may miss an opportunity to address the turnover issue with assessments for hiring.

But there is more. Your sales team must hone their skills so that they can access valuable information not just about buyers' *corporate* strategies and goals, but also about each individual buyer's. Think personal goals versus department and company goals. Think objectives and potential obstacles that may be different from person to person and team to team. The solutions your salespeople offer will be truly value-adding if they can access and address these details.

Personalizing According to Buyer Styles

If your salespeople take the time to document the Decision Pyramid and create a Contact Map of their prospects' and customers' organizations, they will have invaluable tools for spotting and assessing opportunities within the accounts. The next essential tool that should be in every sales team's toolkit is an understanding of Buyer Styles.

As we have discussed, knowing what organizational level a buyer is can give salespeople tremendous insight into what they consider most important in a buying decision. Of course, the factors we have described are generalized based on typical organizational structures and roles. Once you have the opportunity to interact directly with buyers—virtually or in person—you will have access to a wealth of information about each individual based on the behaviors they exhibit.

Today's buyers are more informed and have less time to give to salespeople than ever before. Combine that with the increasingly complex decision-making process, and your salespeople are left with a very narrow opportunity to make a positive connection with a potential buyer.

That is why it is a must for salespeople to be able to quickly identify the buying behavior style of their prospects—and adapt their approach to match.

The fact is, people make purchasing decisions differently. Prospects are far more likely to buy when they unconsciously trust and feel at ease with a salesperson.[63] Building rapport—and ultimately trust—looks different with each buyer behavior style. We find it useful to determine which Buyer Style profile (or combination) each person on our Contact Map appears to be in terms of DISC terminology:

"D" Types

Dominance types are direct and to the point. They typically have fast-paced speech and a strong personality. They tend to think in terms of the bottom line and often have a quicker, more impulsive decision-making style. Salespeople can improve communication with "D" types by:

- Minimizing features—maximizing benefits
- Focusing on how your product or service can help them reach their goals

- Listening closely so they feel they are being heard
- Asking specific, targeted questions and not wasting their time
- Keeping a fast pace to match theirs
- Giving direct answers without a lot of "fluff"

"I" Types

Influence types are friendly and talkative. They typically enjoy interacting with people and like chit chat. Influencers respond well to testimonials and hearing about benefits in an upbeat, positive way. They tend to be less detail oriented, and they focus more on the big picture. You can improve communication with "I" types by:

- Being friendly and animated with your conversation
- Asking for their ideas and opinions
- Not dwelling on the details
- Providing personal stories related to how other people have benefited from your solution

"S" Types

Steadiness types are patient and easy-going. You can identify these individuals by their reserved, indirect, but people-oriented approach to others. They typically have a deliberate and methodical decision-making style and can resist change or anything they perceive as a risk. Salespeople can improve communication with "S" types by:

- Not pressuring them to make a decision quickly
- Listening patiently and taking time to explain
- Speaking with a sincere tone of voice
- Giving direct answers
- Showing you are interested in a long-term relationship

"C" Types

Compliance types are methodical and deliberate. They tend to focus on the details and are primarily concerned about doing things the "right" or "correct way." This buying behavior style can be skeptical and is often concerned with analytics and the effects of change. You can improve communication with "C" types through:

- Presenting data to back up claims about your solution
- Not asking too many personal questions
- Slowing down and precisely answering questions
- Using a diplomatic and courteous tone
- Being conservative in assertions

How to Recognize Behavior Styles

Dominance	Influence
Voice	**Voice**
• Strong, clear, confident, fast-paced, abrupt	• Animated, friendly, rambling explanations
Volume	**Volume**
• Loudest, forceful	• Fairly loud, casual
Body Language	**Body Language**
• Uses direct eye contact	• Smiles a lot
• Points finger	• Expressive gestures
• Leans towards you	• Animated
Email	**Email**
• One or two word responses	• Usually begins with phrases like ... "I hope you are well" or "I hope you are having a good day," etc.
• Short sentences	
• Bullet points	

Steadiness	Compliance
Voice	**Voice**
• Low voice tone, warm, detail-oriented	• Little or no modulation, precise, cool or aloof
Volume	**Volume**
• Soft, methodical	• Quiet volume, deliberate
Body Language	**Body Language**
• Small hand gestures	• Few hand gestures
• Relaxed	• Arms folded
• Steady, easy pace	• Controlled
Email	**Email**
• Personable and lengthy	• Very precise and detailed
	• May be lengthy, usually requesting or referring to data and reports

Personalization in Prospecting: Creating a Compelling Offer

Many salespeople that we talk with begin the initial sales conversation by saying, "Tell me what your problem is, and I can fix it for you." Or worse: "Here is what I do, aren't you interested?" In contrast, what the most successful sales organizations do as they prospect for new business is communicate a deep understanding of what value they bring to organizations or industries. That is what the last section about account planning was all about. If you know what your potential customers need and want, and you have clarity about how your solution(s) meet their goals, you can personalize every conversation you have, leading with your knowledge, making it very clear that you work with similar companies to see improvements in specific areas.

A great way to get ears and doors to open to you is creating compelling offers that incorporate all of that insight. Check out the following example from The Brooks Group—we used this format to make prospecting calls within industries we have a lot of experience in, and it was an effective approach.

Empathetic Statement + Critical Issue	The COVID-19 pandemic has impacted business in previously unimaginable ways, and you likely have found your 2020 sales plan upended. In working with sales leaders in companies like yours, many organizations need to find new opportunities to fill the pipeline through virtual channels.
Proactive Insight	We have been collecting insights from our clients through research and conversations, and we have seen many organizations implementing agile prospecting strategies, such as video outreach, industry re-targeting, and existing account audits.
Meeting Offer	We would like to understand what you are currently doing for prospecting and see if it makes sense to walk you through these insights to see if they help map out how you can address virtual lead generation. Would that make sense?

Let us look at an example crafted by one of our clients:

Empathetic Statement + Critical Issue	We work with casting manufacturers like you to improve product output and reduce downtime for mold cleaning
Proactive Insight	Given our nearly 100 years of business, we have seen thousands of production lines and can usually find two to three ways to help any manufacturer during our first discussion.
Meeting Offer	I would love for you to get a chance to better understand your issues in this area and see if there are some examples that would make sense for you. Would you be available next Friday morning for a 30-minute meeting? I am sure you will find the time valuable.

Most companies train their salespeople on their products, so prospecting sales calls are usually about talking about something "new" or "improved," hoping that the prospect will connect what you do to real problems they are experiencing. The salespeople that can instead speak to the problems they address create a faster connection with the prospect, and if he or she has those issues, the likelihood of a meeting increases—whether the offer is made in person, over the telephone, or through an email. And if your salesperson is seeing customers and prospects every week, in a month they should have gathered critical insights into what the customer set is struggling with, how they are solving the problems, and how your offering can benefit the customer.

Personalization in Sales Calls: Focus on Trust and Value

With the significant increase of virtual meetings, online inventories and ordering, and customer service chat boxes, it is more important than ever for you to deconstruct your sales process so that you use the right communications medium at each step.[64] Seventy-five percent of B2B decision makers are saying now that online and remote selling is equally or more effective for engaging existing customers, and 76% say that online and remote selling is equally or more effective for acquiring new sellers. Sellers and their customers both are getting much more comfortable with interacting with each other via online channels. What used to typically be a half-day face-to-face meeting nowadays may be broken down into a series of phone calls, virtual meetings, text messages, emails, etc. Today's sales professionals must learn how to build rapport and trust with their prospects and customers regardless of the medium in which they are communicating.

A lot of our clients are rethinking what having a relationship with buyers really means. Truthfully, selling really has not changed; the basic selling skills have just been magnified by the need to do so much virtual and hybrid selling. By extension, that means to us that the basic underlying principles behind selling have not really changed, either.

You are really selling only two things: trust and value.

If your buyers need to feel personally "seen and understood" and you are not just approaching them with a one-size-fits-all solution, how can your salespeople imbue every sales interaction with a personalized touch, whether the sales call is virtual or in person? The sales organizations that do that best and most effectively are going to be the teams that succeed in the long run.

Sales professionals thrive off reading body language; they are adept at using certain cues, such as a flinch or a fidget, to their advantage and using the dynamics of the room as data points that make them more effective at closing deals. We still hear salespeople say, "But a sales call *has* to be in person because it is all about relationship building, and I can only build relationships face to face!" Well, it may feel that way—historically, you built relationships face-to-face, but that does not mean it is impossible to do it another way.

In today's hybrid selling environment, how can we ensure humanity remains a part of sales interactions, and how can we be sure our salespeople are picking up on that psychological data which is so critical to the sale?

- **Commanding Attention:** Multitasking is rampant during virtual sales calls. To combat this, encourage your salespeople to ask more questions—probe deeply to get to the heart of the matter. It is perfectly appropriate to query on things like: I would like to make sure I am communicating clearly about my offer—what do you think about it? What do you think of what I said? Do you have any specific concerns about the details of our product or service? Do you mind if I share my screen to show you some visuals around our offer?

- **Interpretation:** Whether the buyer is using the camera or not, now is the time to listen closely to the nuances in their voice—not just what they are saying, but *how* they are saying it. Heightening awareness of those nuances will help your salespeople sharpen their attention and inform a successful response.

- **Focus and Attention:** We all crave attention, and we have all been thrust into situations with unique challenges that affect us in unique ways. It is okay for salespeople to start the call with a little bit of a sympathetic ear—a little kindness can go a long way.

Let us remind you that professional seller-buyer relationships need to be based on trust, not "being liked." Building trust requires a singular focus on what the buyer sees as value.

Recently, we worked with a client who did not clearly understand the value that they could bring to the transaction. Their salespeople would always rush to a lower price because they were afraid their competitor had been talking to the prospect, and they knew they were frequently up against a foreign supplier who was always lower priced. We engaged their salespeople in practicing asking a simple question: "What else have you looked at?" or, "What other solutions have you seen?"

By asking this question of their prospects, they are now opening the door to real conversations that allow buyers to tell them a lot about what they want and need. And the answer to those questions gives them a lot of information about what the buyer VALUES. And it keeps them from feeling forced to offer a significant discount. They have realized a not-insignificant improvement in their gross margins, because now they are just able to ask the question and sell value without fear of pricing. They now understand that it is value that builds relationships.

(By the way, in a Gong.io study of 100,000 sales calls, they found that good salespeople ask more questions and listen longer in a meeting—about 55% of the time—whereas poor salespeople tend to listen only 35% of the time.[65] What do you think is happening when your salespeople listen more? Yes. They are getting more information about what the buyer values.)

Personalization at the C-Level

When you walk into the C-suite, it is a different selling environment. CxO involvement in purchase decisions has specific reasons and necessitates those salespeople have skill sets and knowledge beyond those calling on Layer 2 and 3 customers. Given the pace of change in the 2020s, CEOs are thinking about optimizing their businesses almost as if they are in startup mode, redesigning or redeveloping every process.[66] As a sales leader, you can play an important part in:

- positioning yourself, your team, and your offerings to drive ongoing innovation,
- sharing insights on topics, such as innovation and risk management, with your C-suite contacts to add clarity in the midst of rapid change, and

- helping your customers play offense, strategically.

Consider case studies or insights that you have learned from dealing with your other customers. One of your best sources of information and best positioning tools can be peer-to-peer calls with your own C-suite and your prospects' CxOs. This seems to be a rising trend among top-performing sales organizations: Chorus reported that seller-side C-suite involvement in sales interactions was up nearly 150% in 2020. [67]

The Uncertainty Gap and Looking Ahead

In 2020, we had the opportunity to speak with Sharon Gillenwater, CEO and Co-Founder of Boardroom Insiders, an executive intelligence firm. They create executive profiles with a technology platform designed to help sales and marketing organizations understand what drives C-suite decisions. At the time, one of the things we talked about was what she called the "uncertainty gap." The C-suite—and especially CEOs—at the time were dealing with lingering uncertainty about the true impacts of the pandemic on their businesses.

We believe that for most organizations, the smartest CEOs are always facing an uncertainty gap, knowing that the only constant in the world is change. The pandemic just put this into high relief, forcing even the slowest organizations to ask what the "next normal" will look like. In order to survive the rapid pace of change, great executives in every industry and every part of businesses must be nimble enough to quickly adapt.

> *You are really selling only two things: trust and value.*

The most effective folks in the C-suite make it a practice to strategize about how they need to retool their organizations, their product lines, and their routes to market. They are working to always be a step ahead in anticipating what the market needs right now and also in the foreseeable future. It is important to note that they are not looking at little changes—a better discount on this or better terms here. They are looking for process improvements: How do we do business more effectively? Can it be done in fewer steps? Can I automate part of it? Can part of the transaction be moved online so that the customer can be engaged with it?

Executives are seeking this information and really trying to figure out what the future will look like. In our conversation with Sharon Gillenwater, we spent a lot of time on this question about what C-level individuals now are thinking about. Her view was the thought process was not any different—it is just being performed faster. Five-year planning horizons have become three. Fiscal year plans are now a rolling four or five quarters. Strategic vision has a closer focal point than it used to, and leaders are learning to react and change direction more quickly. Again, that agility thing we keep talking about.

Questions CxOs Need Answered

Top executives make big decisions based on limited information every day. As we have discussed, many executives have personality types that make fast, strong opinions and are impatient with too many details. Ultimately, success or failure with CxO types is based on the salesperson "leading" the conversation, quickly persuading the CxO through their attitude, actions, and questions that they have the company's strategic priorities in focus. These are the questions your C-suite contacts are seeking clarity on. As you and your team strategize effective conversations with these buyers, how would you position your organization, your offerings, and even your sales team to answer them?

- In driving innovation, how do you contribute not just to the small changes, but the big ones?
- How are you helping drive innovation? Improve processes? Automate? Simplify?
- From a sales organizational standpoint, what can you do to help fill that uncertainty gap? Can you bring clarity?
- Can you help shore up an organization's defense, or can you help them play offense by contributing to innovation?

The best way to understand where your customer base is coming from is to ask questions to engage them in conversations at that strategic level. Top performers recognize how they can help their prospects and clients innovate and are part of the buyer's journey— this is how they achieve success.

Biggest Mistakes in Selling to the C-Suite

Wasting the first 3–5 minutes of the call.
Not understanding executives have "discovery fatigue," especially when a lot of questions benefit the seller, not the buyer.
Not understanding that executives have six key performance drives:

1.   *Drive up revenue and profit.*
2.   *Drive down expenses.*
3.   *Drive up market share.*
4.   *Drive down time to market.*
5.   *Drive up retention.*
6.   *Drive down risk.*

Not leading with insights, case studies, and success stories.
Not answering the CxO's first question: "How much should I care?"
Not seeking to understand if any past relationships with your company have created issues with future business.
Not understanding the role of the person you are meeting with and your company—not every vendor deserves time with the CEO.
Not establishing clear next steps (top reps have them 1.53 times more often than average reps).[68]

Personalizing for Procurement

Sellers must make connections within the formal purchasing operation as early in the buying process as possible, ideally when the buyer is first beginning to understand their challenge and explore potential solutions. Salespeople should invite procurement to the table as soon as they identify they will play a role in the decision-making process (even if they are only there to observe.) Through proper questioning, sales professionals can determine where the procurement professional is in the decision-making process, and even walk them backward (if necessary) to make a collaborative diagnosis. They can focus on selling value, instead of responding to a request for a quote or proposal.

B2B Buyer Expectations

There have been a variety of studies exploring changing B2B buyer expectations, and they all seem to center around offsetting risk, adapting to digitalization, and increasing efficiencies. For example, top priorities we have observed for 2021–22 include:

- **Risk management, resilience, and agility; cost savings vs. revenue assurance.** Ninety percent of buyers rated their extended supply network transparency moderate to very low.[69] Many organizations were caught off guard by the pandemic and had little to no insight into availability of their products or the materials needed to manufacture their products. If your organization can support transparency or agility, you have a competitive advantage.

- **Procurement with a purpose; sustainability and social responsibility.** Twenty-nine percent of buyers have required spending amounts with certified sellers.[70] If your organization has sustainability or social responsibility initiatives, this could be a competitive differentiator or a way to create value that is not dependent on your product or service.

- **Technology and digital transformation.** Eighty-seven percent of buyers would pay more for a supplier with an excellent eCommerce portal.[71] This reinforces the idea that buyer preferences toward digital tools have shifted, and for sales organizations that have these capabilities, it is another way to create value beyond the benefits of a product or service.

- **Supply chain diversification.** Offset supplier risk with multiple sources in multiple locations. This may open new opportunities to get into accounts that were monopolized by a competitor, especially if you have locations near the prospect (which reduces transportation costs).

- **Driving value through TCO and operational efficiencies.** This reinforces the importance of long-term value over price, breaking the stereotype for this role. It also represents an opportunity for sales teams to differentiate or create value if they can help procurement accomplish these goals.

Strategies for Purchasing Success

If the purchasing department or a procurement professional is leading the buying process, it is important that sales is in tune with what is driving their decisions. Here are our top five strategies for purchasing success:

Strategy 1. Make procurement relationship connections early—well before there is even a stated need—to develop advocacy with procurement.

Strategy 2. Understand the stakeholders and organizational dynamics of the purchasing decision, including decision makers at all levels.

Strategy 3. Recognize the needs, wants, and priorities of various levels of procurement professionals, beyond just the lowest price.

Strategy 4. Sell and negotiate with transparency, adapting communication approaches and providing resources that align with each contact's preferences.

Strategy 5. Do not discount too quickly. In our survey of procurement professionals, 70% of respondents indicated that they ask for a discount or price concession one to two times before receiving one. This shows that sales has multiple opportunities to communicate and reiterate the value their products or services bring.

Questions Purchasing Professionals Need Sales to Answer

- How does the product/service meet our specifications?
- How does working with your organization mitigate supply chain risk or increase resilience or agility?
- Beyond price, what is the total cost of ownership? How does your offering increase efficiency, save time, etc.? Are there year-over-year savings or financial terms that I can leverage by working with your organization?

- How can you create transparency in the buying process? Are there additional costs (like transportation, freight, etc.) that are not included of which we need to be aware?
- What is the ongoing account service? How accessible is your organization?

Generic Proposals Will Not Cut It

Generic proposals are causing salespeople real problems these days. Prospects expect personalized, customized proposals that show deep understanding of their business opportunities and challenges. Think about it: Your buyers have spent time helping you understand their business and their needs and wants for this transaction. When you present a generic proposal, you are communicating that not only they wasted their time explaining their needs and wants to you, but you were not really listening. Why would you want to do business with someone who breaches your trust so significantly?

But even when we listen, we do not always listen perfectly. Or perhaps the requirements for the purchase have changed. Confirming everything—both at the end of the meeting and before presenting a proposal (if these occur in separate meetings)—is a key component of active listening and confirms in the buyer's mind that your solution will work before they see a price. A prospect usually takes mental possession of your solution before you present price, since that is when they either see themselves succeeding or not with your solution.

> *Top performers recognize how they can help their prospects and clients innovate and are part of the buyer's journey— this is how they achieve success.*

Finally, we have seen a positive response to including a customer's logo or standardized artwork on your proposals. This is a way to again communicate that you are proposing a solution for them, not a generic customer. We have gotten feedback from clients who have noted that our proposals "looked like their organization." We always` try to include a logo, color scheme, and imagery that reflects their industry.

In one case, the client was a professional services firm, and it was difficult to find stock photos that really captured their offerings. So as an alternative, because the company was headquartered in Boston, we included the Boston skyline on the proposal's front page. The client noticed and immediately commented. These touches do make a difference relative to client perception. We will repeat again, though, that just slapping a logo on a presentation alone does *not* make it a personalized sales interaction.

In order to create truly personalized sales interactions with their prospects and customers, today's Hybrid Sellers engage fully in every aspect of the sale. From strategizing about how to win a new account (or new piece of business with an existing customer) and throughout the process of managing and growing profitable accounts, the most successful salespeople are laser focused on what each specific buyer—both the individual and the organization they work for—perceives as valuable. Paying attention to how your company's solutions can address those wants and needs and serving as a guide through the buyer's journey is a recipe for success—but only if your salespeople personalize their interactions with each individual based on the information and decision-making process that are unique to each customer.

Key Takeaways from This Chapter

- When you implement a clear, organized account management program, it enables your salespeople to build strong, value-driven, long-term relationships with customers based on what makes each customer unique. That, in turn, enables them to personalize every sales interaction they have.

- If your salespeople are engaged in conversations only on the bottom two levels of the Decision Making Pyramid, they will seriously face limited opportunities. In contrast, seeking to engage with executive level contacts who are responsible for guiding their companies' strategies and setting goals will allow your salespeople to uncover a far broader range of opportunities.

- Just as organizations and departments have goals, strategies, and tactics, so do the individuals who make decisions on their behalf. Personalizing sales must include an awareness of each individual buyer's approach and needs. There are four primary buyer styles:

- Dominant, "D" types tend to think in terms of the bottom line and often have a quicker, more impulsive decision-making style.
- Influencer, "I" types tend to be less detail oriented, and they focus more on the big picture.
- Steady, "S" types usually have a deliberate and methodical decision-making style and can resist change or anything they perceive as a risk.
- Compliant, "C" types are frequently skeptical and often concerned with analytics and the effects of change.

- Personalization must be integrated into every stage of the buyer's journey (and your sales process), from prospecting to sales calls to customized presentations.

Ask Yourself

- What is unique about each of our top-ten customers? Our top-ten prospects?
- Where is my sales team doing an exceptional job of personalizing sales interactions for and within the organizations to which they are selling? Where could they use improvement, training, and/or support?
- How are we helping our customers drive innovation? Improve processes? Automate? Simplify?
- From a sales organizational standpoint, what can you do to help fill the Uncertainty Gap decision makers have? Can you bring clarity?

CHAPTER 8 FREE TOOL
Selling to Procurement Whitepaper
& Account Management Reality Check

https://brooksgroup.com/download-tools/

Chapter
9

What Makes a Salesperson Successful Today?

If David Bowie's hit, "Changes," is the theme song for sales organizations today, what are the considerations that you as a sales leader need to think about in hiring and equipping salespeople?

Experience in the industry should NOT be the #1 criterion for recruiting new sales team members!

In our work with sales leaders, we find that far too often the number one criterion for recruitment of new sales team members is experience in the industry—and, even better, experience with a direct competitor, selling to the same accounts you want them to sell to in your company. But far too often we see these folks start with a torrent of new prospect meetings, only to quickly fall back into all of the same issues they previously had. As one VP of HR told us, "People looking to move horizontally are usually trying to move to a company without the same problems as their current employer." The reality is you may have different problems than your new hire's old company, but they will soon grow tired of yours as well.

To Make Great Hires, Get Out of Your Own Way First

So, what is a sales leader to do? First, you will likely have to get out of your own way. Most sales managers we know have their own misconceptions about what it takes to be a success in selling, in large part because many sales managers used to be salespeople themselves. If it "worked for me," then it must be right—right? Too often, the boss hires candidates who look just like them, resulting in an organization with similar strengths, but also common flaws.

Next, you will need to confront your own impatience to fill the sales position. We have been there, and it is difficult to take your time, especially when you have goals to beat and the CEO or owner pressuring you to get the team up to full strength. Speed to hire is probably not your friend. There are fantastic sales candidates out there looking for jobs, ready to start immediately, available through no fault of their own. But we like to remember what our company founder used to say: "Hire slow, fire fast," and, "Always be looking for your next hire." Cultivate professional relationships with people outside of your company whose skills and attitude impress you. Keep your eyes out for internal folks who might have what it takes. When you are ready to take your time and be smart about hiring, you will have a list of people—some you have known for months or years, and others who are new applicants—to evaluate and from which to select.

Finally, you will need to implement a selection and hiring process that ensures you choose the right person for the specific sales role you are trying to fill. This will be someone whose behaviors, motivations, and personal skills are in alignment with your company culture and the traits the job requires. At The Brooks Group, we have been committed to full-person hiring for a long time, and we have seen client after client reduce turnover, accelerate time-to-full-performance, and gain new energy in their sales team by broadening the way they look at hiring. In the rest of this chapter, we are going to show you what we have learned about who today's successful sellers are and what characteristics they exhibit.

Is There ONE Top Seller Profile?

Do not get us wrong—anyone *can* be successful in sales. However, every role has a different set of attributes associated with it:

- prospecting versus account management
- transactional versus ongoing sales
- complex buyer decision-making versus a single decision maker

- amount of time inside versus outside
- time spent talking versus time spent updating the CRM

This list is just a small sampling of how sales roles can differ. Knowing what is specific to the sales role(s) at your organization is the first, most important step in building a strong sales team. Ultimately, the goal will be to hire people that fit well into the role, so they can thrive by using their natural strengths. From industry to industry, company to company, and role to role, what is required of an individual in each sales job can widely vary.

The Brooks Talent Index (BTI) is a system of assessments that profile an individual's behaviors, motivators, and clarity around personal and selling skills. In other words, the BTI helps answer this important question: Will their actions, internal drivers, and life experiences make them successful in the job you are looking to fill?

As we mentioned in Chapter 4, the process starts by creating a benchmark for each of the roles you have in your organization. Each benchmark defines the attributes required for success in a given role, within the culture of a specific organization. The sales role at one company may require dramatically different attributes from a job with the same title at a different company with a different product/service or company culture. Once we define these attributes in one of our client's organizations, we generate a set of interview questions, which, in conjunction with each individual's assessment, help the hiring manager understand every candidate's fit for the role and the culture.

The BTI assessments measure the natural behaviors and motivators that each of us formed during childhood and stay fixed unless one experiences significant life challenges and changes. While events such as the pandemic qualify as significant events, our top performer data have shown remarkable consistency across behaviors, motivations, and personal skills.

> *Experience in the industry should NOT be the #1 criterion for recruiting new sales team members!*

There have been a few surprises so far, though—and our best guess is that we do not fully know what the "COVID tax" will be on people in the coming months and years. (We will come back to the surprises in just a bit.)

 THE BROOKS GROUP

Job Attributes Hierarchy

All human jobs require certain people attributes. This section of the report identifies the composite of the respondents to show which attributes are most important to the job in question. Input from all respondents has been averaged. (Details of individual respondents' input are listed in a later section, JOB ATTRIBUTES COMPOSITE). The graphs below are in hierarchical order, from highest to lowest rankings.

1. Customer Focus - A commitment to customer satisfaction.

0 10 20 30 40 50 60 70 80 90 100

79*

92 VI

2. Influencing Others - The ability to personally affect others' actions, decisions, opinions or thinking.

0 10 20 30 40 50 60 70 80 90 100

77*

92 VI

3. Interpersonal Skills - The ability to interact with others in a positive manner.

0 10 20 30 40 50 60 70 80 90 100

79*

86 IMP

4. Goal Achievement - The overall ability to set, pursue and attain achievable goals, regardless of obstacles or circumstances.

0 10 20 30 40 50 60 70 80 90 100

74*

85 IMP

5. Resiliency - The ability to quickly recover from adversity.

0 10 20 30 40 50 60 70 80 90 100

72*

85 IMP

The following scale is used throughout the report.

0 - 4.9	=	NOT IMPORTANT TO JOB
5.0 - 6.9	=	SOMEWHAT IMPORTANT
7.0 - 8.9	=	IMPORTANT
9.0 - 10	=	VERY IMPORTANT

Please note that the population means and standard deviations shown are based on the entire population and are not job/position specific.
* 68% of the population falls within the shaded area.

The BTI assessments are excellent when used as an extra voice in the hiring process as you start to short-list candidates as a way to understand their fit in a role. An assessment is never *the* voice in a hiring decision, but a great tool alongside human interviewers. Plus, the assessment can open new areas of questioning to understand if the sales candidate before you can sell for you, or just sell themselves to you.

What Motivates Top Sales Professionals?

Losing a high-performing employee can have serious effects on your entire team, sales results, and even your sales culture (we mentioned the link between motivators and culture in Chapter 4, too). If you have kept your best folks on board through good times and bad, odds are that they are tired and stressed, even if they are still performing. If they have kept their heads up and their noses to the grindstone during upheaval, how can you keep them to ensure your team regains its equilibrium when the next big change (positive or negative) happens?

One key area to pay attention to is what motivates the individual—it may be multiple things, but what is their strongest motivator? When you look at your company's culture, and compare the individual's motivators to it, is there a match?

With regard to motivators, our top performers, on average, want control of the schedules and financial reward for sales success, with a desire to learn what is important to "get the job done." (In BTI language, they are high Individualistic and Utilitarian, with a Theoretical just above the population mean.) Not really a surprise for salespeople.

This also means they want to control their own destiny, and they will take command of the sales process, invest their time into those activities that generate the highest return, and can manage complex sales environments. These are among the most common motivators that we see in commissioned sales roles. However, they are not the *only* motivators—and folks can be motivated by multiple values, as well.

What Behaviors Do Successful Salespeople Exhibit?

The answer is... it depends on the role and the organization. Behaviorally, the stereotypical top behavioral characteristics are interaction, competitive(ness), and versatility. These are common behavioral traits in our benchmarks for commissioned salespeople—and, in particular, salespeople with responsibility for new account acquisition—and have not really changed over time. (We measure these characteristics using the DISC system we described earlier, and these traits correlate to a D/I or I/D behavior style.) For account managers who work to go "deep and wide" in a customer account, we usually see a higher steady score (the S behavior style).

In certain sales roles—usually selling more technical or complex products—there will be higher adaptations of C scores, which typically reflects some need for more detail, accuracy, or analytical work. (This can also be a result of new processes or systems that require more attention, at least initially.) In other roles, companies look for more I/S behavior styles, especially where working with the same accounts over and over is important, and the salespeople are expected to build deep, long-lasting relationships and understanding of their customers.

Things to Consider in Hiring

(Varies according to role, product/service sold, company culture, and other factors)

- *pace of role*
- *frequency of change*
- *complexity of sale*
- *new relationship building versus existing relationship maintenance and development*
- *salary versus commission pay structure*
- *length of sales cycle*

What Personal Skills Set Salespeople Up for Success?

Personal skills are highly sensitive to the current situation and do change over time. Personal skills measure external and internal clarity. We have anecdotally observed that internal clarity (sense of self, role awareness, and self-direction) for sales teams in general seems to have been lower during the pandemic. Therefore, their scoring on capacities such as resiliency, personal accountability, goal achievement, and self-starting ability has been lower than it was consistently before the pandemic. This would indicate that people came out of the pandemic less sure of their abilities and the fit they have in all of their roles (perhaps a key factor in "The Great Resignation"), and they are more concerned about their long-term plans.

It is worth noting that while these were the lowest skills for our top performers, on average they were still measuring at or above the population mean.

To help illustrate the impact of clarity on personal skills, imagine you are a very good driver—always obeying traffic laws and driving at or below the speed limit. (Yes, hard to believe for sales leaders!) You get word that a loved one has been in an accident and is at a local hospital, not expected to make it. When you jump in the car, the events will overwhelm your safe-driving skills and, you will likely break a number of traffic laws on your way to the hospital.

In the same way, various life events can cause us to question our understanding of people, the tasks we must accomplish as members of society, how clearly we see our personal and professional roles, and even how confident we are in the futures we have planned. All of these directly impact our sales performance.

Our top performers have the highest personal skills scores (called clarity) in empathetic outlook, customer focus, flexibility, influencing others, planning and organization, teamwork, objective listening, and problem solving—all of which likely serve a salesperson well in navigating and adapting to the trends we have discussed in other chapters.

Key Factors for Success in Hybrid Sales

In October 2021, we surveyed sales leaders and asked what specific skills or attributes have been most important to their success since early 2020. From a skills perspective, we heard things such as account planning, call preparation, the ability to expand relationships deeper in client organizations, and adapt questioning strategies to different levels in an organization. In addition, respondents indicated their top performers excelled at virtual communication, setting expectations with clients, and negotiations.

We also heard descriptions of salespeople who exhibited traits like patience, grit, a positive attitude, willingness to adapt, attitude toward change, persistence, mental mindset, continuous improvement, problem solving, and creativity. We even heard a sales leader describe the desire to show up each day and put in the work.

But it is unlikely that a precise list of descriptors perfectly matches the roles you have in sales. Setting up a benchmark and using an assessment tool will help you zero in on the top behaviors, motivators, and personal skills needed for success, since success in sales comes from this combination of inherent traits and trained behaviors and skills. Healthy sales teams start with people who already exhibit the inherent traits they need to benefit from the training, reinforcement, and culture you provide them.

Across the board and over the years, we have been studying such things, it has been consistent that most successful salespeople tend to demonstrate the following traits in varying degrees, depending on the individual and the role:

- **Goal-Oriented.** Salespeople who are strongly motivated by goals are more likely to meet them and, therefore, succeed in the goal-driven environment of sales.
- **Conscientious.** A person who is inclined to be conscientious is more likely to follow up, maintain a consistent prospecting routine, and complete all the tasks necessary to nurture a prospect to a sale.
- **Confident.** Confidence generates trust, enhances rapport, and helps a salesperson continue to perform even under pressure.
- **Supportive Beliefs.** Limiting beliefs, such as, "I don't deserve to make money" or "Salespeople are always sleazy," can hinder performance, while supportive beliefs, such as, "People like me" and "I'm a great presenter," enhance it.
- **Self-Motivated.** A salesperson who comes to work every morning prepared to do everything they need to do and continually improves their skills and performance will always outperform someone who needs sticks and carrots.
- **Teachable/Coachable.** A salesperson who refuses to learn and be coached will never improve as quickly as someone who is willing to listen and learn and apply new sales skills.
- **Cultural Fit.** Your sales culture is one of your most valuable assets. A salesperson whose values conflict with your team's will be a toxic

influence, no matter how good they are at their job. Hire people whose values and beliefs line up with your company's unique culture and reinforce behaviors and attitudes that support it.

- **Flexibility.** What did the pandemic and the other rapid changes of the early 21st century add to the list? If we take resiliency to mean the ability to recover quickly from adversity, then flexibility— the ability to readily modify, respond to, and integrate change with minimal personal resistance—should definitely be on the list. (Historically, our top performers were already relatively high in flexibility, but the trait has taken on even greater importance.)

And now for the surprise—we have recently seen capacities in **planning and organization** rising in top performers' assessments. We were expecting to see flexibility, for all of the reasons we have described so far in this book, but we had not considered that planning and organization might be particularly strong keys to successful selling. While time and a lot more data collection will tell if this trend will be a lasting one, it is definitely another indicator that major events can change attitudes, motivations, and behaviors.

The bottom line is this: If you have the right people on your team—the ones who CAN and WILL do the job—they will be able to connect with buyers effectively and create the personalized experience their buyers demand. In addition, the better they fit into the roles, the greater will be their job satisfaction, resulting in happier team members with lower voluntary turnover.

The Human Touch

Here is another reason to look at behaviors, motivators, and personal skills: The need for focusing on the person in sales has never been higher. This is not because building a friendship with a prospect wins the business, but because building a relationship built on trust is what customers are seeking. And that is ultimately what will win business.

Forrester Consulting asked B2B buyers, "What was the most significant driver of the decision to select the vendor of choice?" comparing the promise of the offering to meet their needs with the influence of customer references or testimonials. In 2015, 17% of respondents chose the promise of the offering to meet their needs, while 11% chose the influence of customer references or testimonials. By 2019, there was a significant change: only 8% of respondents were most influenced by the offering's promise to meet their needs, but 18% put the most weight on customer references or testimonials. Over a four-year period, there was almost exactly a complete switch in prioritization, with far more emphasis now placed on the human element.[72]

What might this tell us? Well, in 2021, after Deloitte commissioned a study from Forrester to answer the question: "What are leading B2B brands doing to close the gap between what buyers expect and what sellers have been doing?" the firm began talking a lot about humanizing B2B experiences. Among the research report's key findings was the measurable, bottom-line impact of connecting with buyers and humanizing interactions: B2B customers are 34% more likely to buy and 32% more likely to renew a contract when they have been treated as a partner through experiences that are "open, connected, intuitive and immediate."[73]

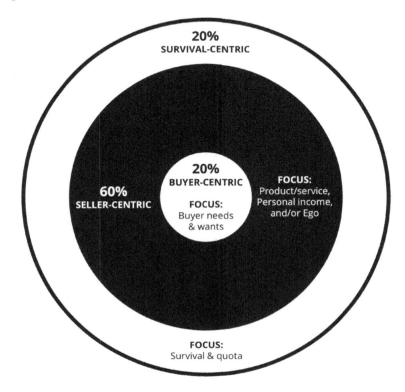

Even today, as digital buying has become a much larger part of B2B selling, research from Gartner shows that customers who make complex purchases without a salesperson end up with higher regrets about the decision.[74] The interaction with a human salesperson in the right places in the flow of the digital buying process is still wanted, improving both the buyer's confidence in the decision and the post-sale satisfaction.

We described in an earlier chapter how the top 20% of sales professionals get their results by focusing on their customer's needs—and the top 10% achieve even greater success by focusing not just on their customer's needs, but also on their customer's wants.

Successful salespeople can access these important details by building deep rapport and lasting trust with their prospects and customers. Before we talk more about the specific skills involved in being able to have a humanized B2B experience, let us talk for a minute about trust.

Building Meaningful Relationships with Prospects and Customers

We define **trust** as your prospect's or customer's belief that you and your organization—and your products or services—are credible and will deliver on every promise or commitment you make. (It did not surprise us in the least that another Forrester study of B2B buyers and sellers listed "trustworthy" at the top of respondents' list of attributes most valued in vendors/partners. "Reliability" came in second.)[75] Developing trust with a prospect or customer is in some ways a no-brainer, but in other ways one of the most challenging aspects of contemporary sales.

It seems commonsensical that we would want to trust the people we are asking to solve essential business problems. Why would anyone invest time and money into a solution—no matter how technically good it seems—if they are not sure the person representing that solution is on the up and up, or knowledgeable enough to represent the solution accurately, or going to ensure implementation of the solution is smooth and effective?

The hard part, though, is getting to the point where prospective customers have the evidence they need to place their trust in your salespeople.

They need to believe that:

- The salesperson's purpose is helping them get the outcomes they need (and want).
- The salesperson generates value for them and their organization.
- The salesperson's organization's products and services promise a lot and deliver even more.
- The investment they are being asked to make in a solution will be lower than the value gained by the solution.
- The salesperson genuinely cares for their company and seeks to connect them with solutions that will reduce their stress, save them money, and otherwise provide a strong ROI.

To build that level of trust with prospects and customers requires emotional intelligence (we will come back to that soon), strong personal skills, excellent sales skills, and a commitment to meeting the buyer where they are in the buying process.

Retention of Great Reps is Priceless

The final benefit of using assessments to find candidates that fit your roles is that the hires will be successful and stick around. We began Chapter 4 with the statistic that 69% of workers say that the pandemic was the most stressful time of their entire professional career, making it more stressful than other major events in this country, such as 9/11 and the 2008 Great Recession.[76] It is worth repeating here because this statistic was reported in the early days of the pandemic—almost 70% of workers were stating this when everyone thought COVID was only going to last a couple of months. The pandemic has affected our jobs, our health, and our relationships, so it is easy to see how it has had a huge impact on our lives, in general.

In 2020, we saw reports that one in four workers are planning to look for new opportunities or seek placement with a new employer once the threat of the pandemic has subsided; but by mid-2021, that number jumped to 55% of the workforce anticipating looking for a new job ("The Great Resignation" everyone talks about).[77]

We say all this not to frighten you, but to remind you that it is worth investing in your salespeople. Coaching is one of the best possible ways to ensure your reps feel seen, encouraged, and valued. Keeping a top performer or building up a B player to become a top performer is, as the commercials say, "priceless."

And here is one more fascinating thing: We read a piece in *Fast Company* in late 2021 in which the CEO of tech firm SailPoint, Mark McClain, predicted that in the near future, the pendulum will swing back, and many employees who left organizations will return. The caveat? It is a big one: This return to work is dependent on the level of trust and the relationships between the company and the employee when they exited.[78] (In other words, it is the culture.)

An Emotionally Intelligent Leader Is a Successful Leader

If your salespeople's traits are affected and influenced by the times, what about yours as a leader? As your teams see Baby Boomers and Gen Xers retire and are replaced with Millennials and individuals from Generation Z, successful sales leaders must become more proficient in understanding and practicing the science of Emotional Intelligence.

Since the 1960s, emotional intelligence (also known as emotional quotient or EQ) has been recognized as a critical component of both personal and professional success. Having a high level of EQ enables a sales leader to better understand and use the power of their emotions during interactions with their team members, executive peers, and customers alike. Understanding and controlling these emotions helps you work through difficult leadership issues, tough business situations, and ensures you maintain trust with all of the parties with which you work.

> *To build that level of trust with prospects and customers requires emotional intelligence, strong personal skills, excellent sales skills, and a commitment to meeting the buyer where they are in the buying process.*

Having a high level of emotional intelligence allows you as a leader to sense, understand, and effectively apply the power of your own emotions during interactions with buyers to improve sales rather than derail them. Often, we all get derailed or distracted by our emotions in the sales process, which can lead to them leaving value on the table, presenting off-target solutions, not asking the right questions or enough questions, or failing to position themselves as a trusted advisor, rather than a nuisance. Or they can fail to have enough awareness in a situation, resulting in a loss of trust, slowing down or losing the sale.

Yet many sales organizations have traditionally focused primarily on building hard sales skills, completely neglecting the importance of emotional intelligence skills. Daniel Goleman, the science journalist who introduced the idea of emotional intelligence in the 1960s, divided EQ skills into five categories:

1. *Self-Awareness.* **The ability to identify and understand one's own emotions and the impact they may have on your actions and on other people.**

   A **self-aware** sales leader is better able to manage their time and energy around their emotional states. They are less likely to anger or annoy a team member or customer with their own negative emotions. And they bounce back from disappointment and rejection faster than those who ignore or are unaware of their negative feelings.

2. *Self-regulation (also referred to as impulse control).* **The ability to control and adapt one's own emotions to fit the situation or to avoid disrupting others.**

   A **self-regulated** sales leader can avoid bringing their negative emotions such as fear, anxiety, or irritation to conversations. They are better able to adapt their behavior to the needs of their job. And they are capable of generating enthusiasm and motivation over the long term to fuel their job performance. They are also less likely to fire off that angry email, storing the first version in drafts until they are able to more diplomatically write.

3. *Social Skills.* **The ability to have social awareness, make meaningful connections, build rapport, and maintain relationships over an extended period of time.**

   A professional sales leader with strong **social skills**, which we at The Brooks Group refer to as *Social Awareness*, will be successful at networking and leading because they are able to maintain a larger, stronger network from which to draw sales opportunities and potential team recruits. They will be good at collaborating and cooperating with their peers. And they will know how to "read a room" and adjust their own behavior to get the outcomes they desire.

4. *Empathy.* **The ability to identify and understand other people's emotions, and the desire to respond to them productively (the counterpoint to self-awareness).**

An **empathetic** sales leader is good at judging how the person (customer, peer, employee) is feeling, so that they can adapt their approach and steer conversations in the right direction. At The Brooks Group, we refer to this as *Social Regulation*. Empathy also helps the sales leader visualize the person's experience to better understand their needs, their goals, and their pain points so that they can address them in the most effective way.

Note: For a sales leader to be effective, their empathy levels should not be too low *or* too high. Too much empathy can cause one to be overly sensitive to the feelings of others, potentially making them avoid asking difficult questions about the decision dynamics in an account or other hard questions because they feel the other person may find it rude, pushy, or confrontational.

5. *Motivation.* **The internally generated desire to complete a task or accomplish a goal.**

Sales leaders with strong **motivation** get more done in a day. They respond better to frustration and seek out opportunities to improve their skills. They embrace new behaviors and activities that help them reach their goals. They listen to coaching and apply it to their work. And they pursue coaching their team for improvement more assertively than their peers.

Together, these five emotional intelligence skills comprise the building blocks of a healthy, productive approach to life and work. Emotionally intelligent sales leaders perform better than their non-emotionally intelligent peers. (Our research and that of others has consistently shown this.) Emotional Intelligence is partly an innate, naturally acquired set of traits, but the skills associated with it can be developed to improve your sales team's performance.

And once you have grown in your EQ, you are ready to help your team discover and master their EQ through effective coaching. That is what the next chapter is all about.

When we talk about motivators in hiring and coaching (relative to the BTI) we refer to external motivators, which is the drive for money, service, power, knowledge, etc. Motivation as it relates to EQ is internal—it is a passion to work that goes beyond the external. Internal/intrinsic motivation can be the most powerful driver of performance. This is more of an internal persistence that propels an individual regardless of emotional temperature.

Key Takeaways from This Chapter

- To make great hires, sales leaders must do three things:

  1. Get out of their own way, confronting and rejecting any misconceptions they have about the sales role.
  2. Relax their own attitude and sense of urgency about filling the role.
  3. Systematize a hiring and selection process that successful candidates' behaviors, motivations, and personal skills are in alignment with your company culture and the traits the job requires.

- Healthy sales teams start with people who already exhibit the inherent traits they need to benefit from the training, reinforcement, and culture you provide them. Most successful salespeople tend to demonstrate these traits in varying degrees, depending on the individual and the role:

  1. Goal-oriented
  2. Conscientious
  3. Confident
  4. Supportive beliefs
  5. Self-motivated
  6. Teachable/coachable
  7. Cultural fit

8. Flexibility
9. Planning and Organization

- The need for focusing on the person in sales has never been higher. This is not because building a friendship with a prospect wins the business, but because building a relationship built on trust is what customers are seeking.
- The most successful sales professionals exhibit exceptional emotional intelligence, strong personal skills, excellent sales skills, and a commitment to meeting the buyer where they are in the buying process.
- Emotionally intelligent sales leaders perform better than their non-emotionally intelligent peers. They have stronger skills in five key areas:

1. Self-Awareness
2. Self-Regulation
3. Social Skills
4. Empathy
5. Motivation

Ask Yourself

- How have I "gotten in my own way" in making hiring decisions? What can I do differently now that I know more?
- Knowing that a successful salesperson is different at varying companies and in different industries, what are some of the behaviors and motivations that salespeople exhibit who are successful at my company?
- How can I grow and intentionally develop my own EQ?

CHAPTER 9 FREE TOOL
Ultimate Guide to Hiring Quota-Smashing Sales Reps
Whitepaper & Style Audit

https://brooksgroup.com/download-tools/

Chapter

10

Great Sales Leaders Serve Their Teams

There is something different about being a sales leader. While all managers have metrics to achieve, only in the sales leadership role do you compete with those external to your organization. Engineering and finance are measured in relation to internal factors—measures such as quality, accuracy, and delivery. Sales is measured on internal factors, too, such as order accuracy, following procedures, and even non-measurable metrics like getting along with marketing. However, your sales team's performance is also measured by the market against external factors outside of your control.

While your team bears the weight of the financial health of your company, there is the need to meet the all-important Number that keeps the company profitable and, in many cases, keeps the stock price rising. You also frequently have your hands tied by quality and delivery issues, by waiting for new product collateral and samples, or customer service problems. Sales is at the mercy of every other department.

Great sales leaders serve as the hub of a vast network of stakeholders.

As a sales leader, you must be able to select which messages get passed along, as well as how—up, down, and laterally within your organization. This sometimes happens even *to* and *with* your customers. You must be able to drive progress toward reaching the Number by engaging your sales team and other resources effectively in service of your company's mission.

Think about the coach of a professional NBA team. Balancing the demands of the team's owners with the needs of the players is a way of life, and you can be sure you will hear from the team's fans, too. As a sales leader, you are in a similar position. Teaching yourself to be a coach—not a manager—of your reps will not only get better results, but will also buy you the time you need to strategize. Sure, coaching takes effort, and it can feel like you are adding time-consuming activities to your already busy days. But by investing your time (and that is what it is, *investing*) in coaching and systematizing high-gain activities, you will end up with more resilient, capable salespeople who know how to get results that yield the Number you are ultimately accountable for hitting.

Two Critical Reasons for Sales Coaching

The top 30% of reps outperform the bottom 30% by as much as four times.[79] Imagine if you could close that performance gap—even just a fraction—between your stronger and weaker performers. That is just one reason why your role as a sales coach is so important.

The other? Change management has become one of the most essential skills for sales leaders in recent years. Fifty-two percent of sales organizations have experienced a high degree of change this decade, and 56% expect extensive changes to continue, yet only 36% say sales management has effectively prepared their sales team to adapt and change.[80]

While their sales teams complain about lack of support and development, most sales leaders rate themselves very highly in terms of effective formal coaching. They are likely overly confident because it seems less than 25% of sales managers have implemented a formal coaching program for their teams.[81] That is a real problem, yet solving it can have positive results. Companies that use sales behavior insights—such as joint call audits, ride alongs, and weekly call reports—improve productivity by 20%.[82]

What would 20% greater productivity look like for your team? What would 20% greater productivity mean to your team? To your company? To you?

After completing our IMPACT Selling courses, clients committed to lasting change engage us to coach their teams over a few months as they implement IMPACT. In nearly every session, right around the third or fourth week, someone who previously did not believe in following a sales process or utilizing one of the sales skills we teach will say something like, "When I heard this at first, I didn't believe it would work. But I tried it [which could be asking a deeper discovery question, adapting their behavior closer to the prospects, or even holding firm on the initial price quoted on a proposal] and, wow, it worked." Coaching gave the individual time (and perhaps peer pressure) to experiment with change, and sharing their results will help the change stick for them as well as their peers.

Why Is Sales Coaching So Hard?

It is kind of like flossing. Everyone knows they should do it more often than they actually do it. We have observed thousands of sales organizations over our 40-plus years at The Brooks Group, and we have heard it all. The most common reasons for *not* coaching are perceived lack of time, lack of knowledge, and lack of confidence. We've noticed something interesting, though. Think about this and be very honest with yourself when you react.

In our Sales Leadership programs, we often ask, "Do you believe you're the best salesperson in your organization?" Between 60% and 70% of these leaders consistently raise their hands. So many managers would rather get in and win the deal, loving that feeling of "closing." But the rest of the team does not develop and they get discouraged because they

> *Great sales leaders serve as the hub of a vast network of stakeholders.*

are not getting full credit for the deal. Plus, every day, every interaction other than the one the manager is engaged in is sub-par. And that means overall results are sub-par as well.

Here is a real important Sales Leadership Truth: Most of you are good at, and take the time to, deal coach—the act of helping a salesperson close the deal. What we are talking about here is skills coaching, the single most important job of the sales manager. If your team is going to be successful (and you are going to be successful) in the long-term, it is because your team knows how to perform well, having the right degree of autonomy and the ability to make good decisions.

So, when we jump in to "save" sales calls when our salespeople stumble, what are we really accomplishing? Sure, we may help on that one call, but we would get a lot more bang for our buck if we enabled salespeople to do better the next time and the time after that and the time after that. That is what coaching is all about. It is kind of like the old adage, "Give a man a fish, and he'll eat tonight; teach a man to fish, and he'll eat for the rest of his life."

Years ago, we were working with the sales leaders at a business services company. The company had incredibly high turnover among salespeople, which was a concern. As we spent more time with them, we discovered that the first-level sales managers actually saw themselves in competition with their own salespeople. They tried to grab the best leads and were so insecure they had to finish every month as the top producers. Conversations followed with the executives of the company. Ultimately, they decided to restructure the organization, with clearer role definition between first-tier managers and salespeople. Managers grasped that their job was team performance, not competition.

The best kind of coaching—and the most rewarding for managers and their salespeople—is mentoring. In essence, you are working with the salesperson training them for their next job, which might eventually include replacing you. So many of us in management initially struggle with the fear that if you train people to be leaders, they will leave. But retention rates actually go *up more than 50%* because people feel you really have their interest at heart.[83] In addition, you build a stronger bench that makes your promotion easier for corporate, and in the meantime gives you a chance to delegate certain tasks—growing their skills and freeing up your time.

Every sales leader we talk to has one or two big frustrations with their team and keeps saying, "We've got to get better." But all too often, they fail to take steps toward improvement, which means they have a problem with coaching or a problem with replacing salespeople who are not performing.

It is amazing how often we are asked, "I've tried a number of different approaches to fixing my team, but nothing works. What do you think is the problem?" It is always a difficult conversation to help them realize their personal failure to manage is likely the cause.

Another Sales Leadership Truth: You own this. Coaching is yours. As the leader of this team, you set and communicate clear standards.

This sounds so basic, but here is the type of conversation we frequently have with sales leaders:

- **Sales Lead:** The weakness we have is that they are not finding new business.
- **The Brooks Group:**
    - How are you encouraging them to do that?
    OR
    - How does the comp plan align with new business?
    OR
    - What is the penalty if they do not get new business?
- **Sales Lead:** Well, I have *told* them it's important.

Those sales leaders have not set standards for the organization or they have not held their people accountable for the standard. In the next section, we will share some of our best coaching advice, but first let us look at where those standards should be generated.

Types of Coaching That Work

Sales coaching, in a nutshell, is the ongoing, individualized teaching and guidance on the part of sales managers to improve salesperson performance. Coaching tends to fall into three categories:

- Deal Coaching: How do we win this particular opportunity?
- Sales Skills Coaching: What do you need to do to perform in the role you are in?
- Digital Coaching: How do we use digital tools effectively to win sales?

As we described in an earlier chapter, our Brooks Talent Index (BTI) system provides integrated, effective tools for benchmarking, hiring, and performance management. However, there are plenty of ways to systematize this part of coaching.

One approach we have seen work is establishing a key accountability matrix. Start with the job description for your sales role and highlight the top four or five things—no more than that—you want your team to be doing. List those four or five things, then assign to each both a priority ranking and a percentage of time you think should be spent on each area. For example, let us say you prioritized "finding new business" as number one—should reps be investing 20% or 50% of their time into those efforts?

Key Accountabilities for Your Sales Role

Position Title: Territory Sales Representative

Key Accountabilities	Priority/Rank	Weight
A. Prospecting; generate new opportunities to maintain pipeline	1	30%
B. Close sales; meet sales targets	2	30%
C. Collaborate internally and externally; manage client relationships and work with team members	3	20%
D. Maintain knowledge of products, industry, competition, and customer base	4	15%
E. Problem solving, critical thinking	5	5%

Beginning with this simple tool gives you a baseline to communicate expectations and then assess performance, and you can coach your salespeople within the context of the matrix. We will talk more about that in just a bit. Let us start with a look at the three most effective ways our client sales leaders provide coaching to their teams—and the individuals on them.

Group Coaching

If you have a group of people all missing or struggling with similar skills—such as communication of expectations, how to discuss when deadlines overlap, how to use a new digital tool, or how to think from a customer's perspective—you can set aside a part of each team meeting to work on a designated skill area. For instance, if your team meets weekly, then you can address a skill each week. If you make it a consistent part of your sales meetings, it can take as little as ten minutes to focus on something the entire group needs. Think about who on your team is doing well in a particular skill area and let them present on it—not content you create, but their own presentation. This gives the salesperson a chance to stand in front of their peers and be recognized as strong in that area, and it sets the stage for peer-to-peer coaching (where you pair people up to share and learn from each other's strengths).

> *Sales coaching, in a nutshell, is the ongoing, individualized teaching and guidance on the part of sales managers to improve salesperson performance.*

One-on-One Coaching

One-on-one coaching is for targeting areas of individual need. Each person is different, and obviously we each have various strengths and weaknesses. In one-on-one coaching, a leader can work with a team member on specific issues, not only for improvement of weaknesses, but also for accelerating unique strengths. Russ once worked with an incredibly gifted salesperson who moved into sales management. But this person's ability to manage (and coach) needed growth before he could really flourish. That kind of focus can only be done one-on-one. In the next section, we will look at our top ten coaching principles in detail.

Peer Mentoring Coaching

One of the advantages of peer mentoring coaching is it can multiply your coaching capacity. We see a couple of really key advantages here. First, you get the chance to let experts in certain areas share that expertise. Have someone great at building executive relationships? Let them coach others. You probably have someone on your team who is great at prospecting, generating referrals, or any other sales skill—even something as critical and hard as forecasting. Set up a formal process for peer mentoring, and encourage informal coaching relationships.

There is frequently a chance for productive cross-generational coaching. During the rapid movement to virtual selling during the pandemic, we had a client who paired younger and older salespeople—the older ones coached on sales skills, the younger ones worked on how to improve digital skills. Studies have shown that millennials lean into peer coaching quickly, wanting to teach and not just be an apprentice to anyone.

The Brooks Group's Top 10 Coaching Principles

As a leader, you cannot force anyone to be accountable for their responsibilities. You cannot make them do anything they do not want to do. What you *can* do is create a work environment that facilitates their high performance, providing the necessary resources, giving clear feedback, offering coaching where it is needed or requested, and holding them accountable for the results. We get it, though: Your ability to collaborate effectively with your team and guide your people to achieve their goals is more important and more difficult than ever.

Coaching Principle 1: Coaching must be consistent.

Schedule the sessions as early in the day, as early in the week, and as early in the month as possible. We all know how the days (and weeks and months) get away from us as sales leaders. The closer it gets to the end of our financial reporting period, the harder it is going to be to find the time.

If you tell somebody you are committed to their improvement, you need to demonstrate that by making it a priority in your calendar.

Coaching Principle 2: Coach A, B, and C players differently.

The B players are the best investment—you typically get the most increases in results through coaching them. For the C players, consider whether their issues are because they cannot do the job, or will not do the job? Depending on your observations, you should determine if it is going to be worth investing your time into the player. The A players need coaching, too—do not forget that. They are more likely to remain on your team and deliver great results if they believe you are investing in them.

Coaching Principle 3: Have a very clear agenda for coaching.

Change will not happen all at once, so write down the plan so you both can track progress. Mutually create SMART goals or use some other mechanism so that follow-up is clear and simple. There should be no question whether they accomplish a goal or not. (Sometimes people fear you are going to send the plan to HR. Be clear this is not the case, and that the coaching sessions are between the two of you—unless, of course, the problem reaches that point. And even then, communicate why you are sending a copy to HR.)

Coaching Principle 4: Guide, don't dictate.

Your salespeople should feel that you are investing in them and actively wanting their success—not just because you are the sales leader, but because you value them as human beings capable of great things. Self-discovery is really the way in which an individual recognizes a gap and takes action to improve it. Getting their input and buy-in is essential. (Tip: Asking, "Would you like my opinion?" opens doors and removes some resistance, but only after they have had a chance to speak and come up with their own ideas.)

Coaching Principle 5: Model questioning.

You, as a sales coach, need to model asking great open-ended questions. The coaching journey requires discovery in the same way the sales process does. In this way, you are coaching on both operational issues and deal coaching at the same time. "What's working right now for you and what is not?" "What are you doing differently now than you were doing six months ago when you were way above plan?" "How do you feel you could improve to win more?" "How do you develop or measure good relationship?"

Coaching Principle 6: Gather data using tools that track with your selling system.

In addition to improving results, using a selling system provides a common language with your sales team so you have objective ways to identify challenges, measure in-process results, and coach in real time. Be sure your assessment tools for gathering data align with the steps and priorities of your selling process. Data analytics sounds like a big deal, but it is actually quite simple: Look at the data you have. Something as routine as weekly call reports tell you who is making calls and what their number of prospects looks like. Track that over a period of time and you have a lot of insight into where areas of challenge lie. Start *somewhere* with what is easily available to you. If you can incorporate technology later on, or do more sophisticated research, great. But honestly, just paying attention to the basics yields results.

Coaching Principle 7: Make the human connection.

If you are meeting in-person, use what you know of the salesperson's behavior style and motivators to communicate most effectively with him or her. If you are coaching remotely, always use video. Facial expressions add a lot to communication and help both parties to better understand each other, as well as to communicate fully and openly. Do not record the session. People get very concerned that recordings will get shared. One important note—if you are coaching remotely, be sure to leave a little extra time to make a human, personal connection before the coaching call starts.

Coaching Principle 8: Stay engaged from a position of self-awareness.

Sales leaders who are self-aware understand their own tendencies, how they come across, and how to effectively read and communicate with others. "Own" part of the coaching process yourself with your strengths and weaknesses in mind. When together you come up with a coaching plan for someone, try to develop some tasks that you are going to own and do—and that you can realistically do well—so they can see you are committed to their improvement. Then, really do them!

Coaching Principle 9: Give them an early win.

Nobody likes to feel like they are spinning their wheels—we all need encouragement when we are trying to learn a new skill or make change. For example, let us say your salesperson is going to try something new in sales calls. Have them text you the next couple of days every time they do a call to tell you what they have really accomplished. That text reinforces the behavior, and it gives you a chance to cheer them on.

Coaching Principle 10: Know when it is just not working.

All leaders hate it when we get to this point. Whether out of a loyalty to a person or a sense that we are all supermen or superwomen and can get anyone on track, too often we do not recognize when we have hit a wall. When you acknowledge that you are really dealing with a *won't do*, as a leader you need to, as dispassionately as possible, do what is best for the organization (and your whole team) and seek to have the individual you are coaching put into another role—inside or outside your organization.

Russ had an experience that illustrates the importance of this principle well:

> *"I once took over a team from a leader who had been with the company for 19 years. This individual rarely met deadlines and had a hard time understanding the real business issues in a situation. We worked through a couple of quarters of coaching, mutually setting clear expectations and talking through the results. When he continued to miss the mark, I let him go.*
>
> *I learned two important lessons: First, I was afraid that the organization would greatly miss his 19 years of experience. What I found was that other people stepped up with more energy, commitment to deadlines, and business insights. Never once did we say, 'We need his help on this.' Second, multiple team members communicated that they were glad he was gone and asked why it took me so long to make the decision. My best team member even went so far as to say about six months later that, 'If he had stayed a part of the organization, I would probably have moved on.' Your team recognizes underperformers a lot faster than you do sometimes. They will value your steps to improve the team."*

Next Steps to Consider

Big changes are not going to happen today or overnight. As a sales leader, you need to be in it for the long haul, celebrating incremental wins that will add up to major change in the long run. We are aware, though, that you need to see improvements and see results sooner rather than later. Consider the following questions as you plan the next steps in your sales leadership journey:

1. **Is your sales team prepared for ongoing change? Are agility and resiliency embedded into your sales organization's culture?**

    -   Your salespeople must be supported and empowered to anticipate and accommodate the rapid pace of change. This requires a focus on the total culture of your organization, not just individuals' skill levels and team sales results. If your culture is strong, it builds commitment to you and your organization.
    -   It is important to balance the KPIs you use between outcome-based and in-process metrics in order to focus your team on the behaviors that drive excellent results.
    -   Structure your sales team so each person has a clearly defined role and responsibilities, enabling your people to deliver the personalized service their customers expect.

2. **In a buyer-centric world, are your B2B salespeople fully aware that buyers have changed the rules of engagement?**

    -   Customer expectations have been set by B2C experiences, so B2B sales leaders must invest in digital tools that allow self-service for buyers—but also position their salespeople to add value at critical points in the buyer's journey.
    -   Coaching your sales team to learn and help guide the buying process will differentiate them in a market with aggressive price competition and an overabundance of "thought leadership."

3. **Does every member of your sales team have what it takes to be a powerfully effective Hybrid Seller?**

   - If your team's general attitude is "we'll get back to normal any day now," it is time to take another look. The massive changes in B2C and B2B commerce in recent years are not going anywhere—many were underway before the pandemic hit.
   - Practicing creating a Value Formula for each potential sale is time well spent. Make this a subject for your weekly team meeting and ensure that every salesperson's focus is on what value they and your company's products/services bring to their prospects and customers.
   - Account planning and management are essential skills for today's Hybrid Sellers. If this is not your strength, get outside help to coach your team. It makes a direct impact on how able your salespeople are to sell value.

4. **Are you prepared to grow and/or build a sales team ready for success?**

   - Is your team set up for integrated team selling? If not, begin redefining roles, reorganizing your team, and training across the board so that your customers can have a consistent experience across every touchpoint.
   - If you are not benchmarking the sales roles required today, get that process started right away. Then, evaluate your existing salespeople against the benchmark.
   - If you have open positions, evaluate any potential hires against the benchmark. Remember to always be on the lookout for potential top salespeople, even when you are not actively hiring.
   - You "own" the job of coaching your team. If you are feeling overwhelmed or under-skilled, get help. (Shameless self-promotion: That is what The Brooks Group is here for!)

May the Odds Be Ever in Your Favor

Throughout this book, we have focused on our belief that the next era of sales will demand companies continually improve their innovation and problem-solving capabilities. Research and our observations routinely point to the ongoing need for sales professionals to take the driver's seat in improving the buyer/seller relationship. The way forward for us as salespeople is addressing areas truly valued by our customers, who are simultaneously wanting to be more in control *and* have more personalized interaction from salespeople with whom they choose to interact. We anticipate that the speed of change will stay consistently rapid in the coming years, and the sales teams that are best equipped to anticipate and respond to it will thrive no matter what comes their way.

Here's to your sales success!

CHAPTER 10 FREE TOOL
Coaching Session Planner

https://brooksgroup.com/download-tools/

References

* Goldsmith, Marshall, What Got You Here Won't Get You There (New York, NY: Hyperion, 2007).

1 "Excellence Sought—And Found," Forbes, Oct 4, 2002, accessed online at https://www.forbes.com/2002/10/04/1004excellent.html?sh=12f7863212af.

2 Bradley, Chris. "Surprise: Those 'Great' Companies Generally Turn out to be Meh...or Duds." MarketWatch online. 31 August 2017. Accessed online at: https://www.marketwatch.com/story/great-companies-are-more-likely-to-do-really-badly-over-time-than-really-well-2017-07-12.

3 "Creating Greater Agility: The Essential Influence of the C-suite," Project Management Institute (PMI) and Forbes Insights, 2017.

4 Nink, Marco. "How to Weave Agility throughout Your Corporate Culture," Gallup Workplace, 17 January 2019.

5 Lawrence, Barry. "Organizations Are Getting Agile, But Not Quickly Enough," Human Resource Certification Institute (HRCI): 12 June 2018.

6 "The Next Era of Human/Machine Partnerships: Emerging Technologies' Impact on Society and Work in 2030," Institute for the Future (IFTF) and Dell Technologies: 2017. Accessed online at https://www.delltechnologies.com/content/dam/delltechnologies/assets/perspectives/2030/pdf/SR1940_IFTFforDellTechnologies_Human-Machine_070517_readerhigh-res.pdf.

7 Sales Management Association, Executing Hard Pivots in Sales Strategy, 27 Oct. 2020.

8 Shea, Mary, et al. "The Democratization of B2B Sales: Talent Wins Games, But Teamwork and Intelligence Win Championships." Forrester Research, Inc. 3 August 2020.

9 Nanji, Ayaz. "10 Interesting B2B Marketing Stats [Infographic]." Accessed online at: https://www.marketingprofs.com/chirp/2021/45156/10-interesting-b2b-marketing-stats-infographic.

10 Campbell, Colin. "What Is the Buyer's Journey? (And Why It Matters). Sales Hacker online. 7 July 2021. Accessed online at: https://www.saleshacker.com/buyer-journey/.

11 "New B2B Buying Journey & Its Implication for Sales." Gartner. Accessed online at: https://www.gartner.com/en/sales/insights/b2b-buying-journey.

12 Bages-Amat, Arnau, et al. "These Eight Charts Show How COVID-19 Has Changed B2B Sales Forever," McKinsey & Company, 14 October 2020. Accessed online at: https://www.mckinsey.com/business-functions/marketing-and-sales/our-insights/these-eight-charts-show-how-covid-19-has-changed-b2b-sales-forever.

13 Paris, Costas, and Stella Yifan Xie. "COVID-19 Closure at China's Ningbo Port is Latest Snarl in Global Supply Chains." The Wall Street Journal. 20August 2021. Accessed online at: https://www.wsj.com/articles/covid-19-closure-at-chinas-ningbo-port-is-latest-snarl-in-global-supply-chains-11629451800?st=z9ab06za7jau002&reflink=desktopwebshare_permalink.

14 Campbell, Colin. "What Is the Buyer's Journey? (And Why It Matters)." Sales Hacker online. 7 July 2021. Accessed online at: https://www.saleshacker.com/buyer-journey/.

[15] 2017 Gartner Digital B2B Buyer Survey.

[16] Gartner webinar, Sales Leadership Vision 2022, 18 October 2021.

[17] Nauck, Fritz, et al. "The Resilience Imperative: Succeeding in Uncertain Times." McKinsey & Company, 17 May 2021.

[18] "The Competitor: Jack Welch's Burning Platform," InformIt online. 5 September 2003, accessed online August 2021 at https://www.informit.com/articles/article.aspx?p=100665.

[19] Guglielmo, Connie. "The Steve Jobs Deal with Michael Dell that Could Have Changed Apple and Tech History," C-net online. 6 October 2021. Accessed online at: https://www.cnet.com/tech/computing/the-steve-jobs-deal-with-dell-that-could-have-changed-apple-and-tech-history/.

[20] TOPO Research/Gartner, Virtual Summit, April 30, 2021.

[21] You can check it out here (https://www.Gong.io/blog/women-are-way-better-than-men-at-this-high-value-sales-skill/) if you would like to read more.

[22] As quoted in the Wall Street Journal, October 20, 2018.

[23] O'Gara, James. "So, You Want to Be a Thought Leader." *Texas CEO Magazine* online, 2 March 2021.

[24] Remember, when we refer to *buyer*, we mean any decision-maker involved in making the choice to commit to, or purchase, a B2B product or service.

[25] Dickie, Jim, and Barry Trailer, "2021: State of Buyer & Seller Engagement—The 'New' New." 2021, Sales Mastery LLC and Korn Ferry.

[26] "Forrester's B2B Summit Kicks Off; New Research Reveals COVID-19 Pandemic Dramatically Altered B2B Buying Behaviors." Press Release, 4 May 2021. Accessed online at: https://www.forrester.com/press-newsroom/forresters-b2b-summit-kicks-off-new-research-reveals-covid-19-pandemic-dramatically-altered-b2b-buying-behaviors/.

[27] Nanji, Ayaz, "10 Interesting B2B Marketing Stats" Infographic. 22 June 2021. Accessed online https://www.marketingprofs.com/chirp/2021/45156/10-interesting-b2b-marketing-stats-infographic.

[28] Apollo, Bob. "Understanding Your Customer's Decision Journey." The Outcome-Centric Selling Blog. Inflexion Point. 28 November 2019.

[29] Dickie, Jim, and Barry Trailer, "2021: State of Buyer & Seller Engagement—The 'New' New." 2021, Sales Mastery LLC and Korn Ferry.

[30] Mayer, Kathryn. "HRE's Number of the Day: Coronavirus Stress," Human Resource Executive online, 14 April 2020.

[31] Prudential Financial's Pulse of the American Worker survey, conducted by Morning Consult, September 2021. Accessed online October 2021 at: https://news.prudential.com/prudential/research-and-perspectives/american-workers-survey/.

[32] Thompson, Derek. "The Great Resignation Is Accelerating," *The Atlantic*. 15 October 2021.

[33] Pophal, Linda. "Top 6 Reasons People Are Quitting Their Jobs (and How to Keep Them)," Outsmart blog, accessed online November 2021 at https://www.visier.com/blog/trends/top-6-reasons-people-are-quitting-their-jobs-and-how-to-keep-them/.

[34] "4 in 5 Employees Want Benefits or Perks More Than a Pay Raise; Glassdoor Employment Confidence Survey (Q3 2015)." Glassdoor. 2 October 2015. Accessed online November 2021 at https://www.glassdoor.com/blog/ecs-q3-2015/.

[35] Groysberg, Boris, et al. "Guide to Corporate Culture: How to Manage the Eight Critical Elements of Organizational Life." Harvard Business Review. January-February 2018.

[36] Smith, Rick. "The State of SAS: After 5 Years of Flat Revenue, Growth May Be Returning in 2021," WRAL TechWire. 18 May 2021. Accessed online in October 2021 at https://www.wraltech-wire.com/2021/05/18/the-state-of-sas-after-5-years-of-flat-revenue-growth-may-be-returning-in-2021/.

[37] Groysberg, Boris, et al. "Guide to Corporate Culture: How to Manage the Eight Critical Elements of Organizational Life." Harvard Business Review. January-February 2018.

[38] Chatman, Jenny, and Francesca Gino. "Don't Let the Pandemic Sink Your Company Culture." Published on HBR.org. 17 August 2020.

[39] Chatman, Jennifer; David F. Caldwell, et al., "Parsing Organizational Culture: How the Norm for Adaptability Influences the Relationship Between Culture Consensus and Financial Performance in High-Technology Firms," *Journal of Organizational Behavior*. Wiley Online Library. Published online 11 April 2014.

[40] Chatman, Jennifer; David F. Caldwell, et al., "Parsing Organizational Culture: How the Norm for Adaptability Influences the Relationship Between Culture Consensus and Financial Performance in High-Technology Firms," *Journal of Organizational Behavior*. Wiley Online Library. Published online 11 April 2014.

[41] Riley, Craig, and Brent Adamson, "The Gartner Chief Sales Officer's Leadership Vision: Win in 2022," Gartner webinar, 2021.

[42] Moran, Sean, and Amy Myers. "Five Ways that Middle-Market Companies Use KPIs to Drive Higher Performance," ZS Associates online. 6 October 2020. Accessed online at: https://www.zs.com/insights/five-ways-that-middle-market-companies-use-kpis-to-drive-higher-peformance.

[43] Chappuis, Bertil, et al. "The Domino Effect: How Sales Leaders Are Reinventing Go-to-Market in the Next Normal," McKinsey & Company, 1 October 2020. Accessed online at: https://www.mckinsey.com/business-functions/marketing-and-sales/our-insights/the-domino-effect-how-sales-leaders-are-reinventing-go-to-market-in-the-next-normal.

[44] Osman, Maddy, "The Most Important Sales KPIs to Track for Measuring Sales Success," Cirrus Insight, 19 August 2020. Accessed online at: https://www.cirrusinsight.com/blog/sales-kpis.

[45] "Reinvent B2B Selling for Digital Environment," Gartner webinar, 27 September 2021.

[46] Zoltners, Andris A., PK Sinha, and Sally E. Lorimer. "4 Questions Sales Leaders Should Be Asking Right Now," Harvard Business Review. 3 June 2020. Accessed online August 2021 at https://hbr.org/2020/06/4-questions-sales-leaders-should-be-asking-right-now https://hbr.org/2020/06/4-questions-sales-leaders-should-be-asking-right-now.

[47] Zoltners, Andris A., PK Sinha, and Sally E. Lorimer, "4 Things Sales Organizations Must Do to Adapt to the Crisis," *Harvard Business Review*. 13 April 2020. Accessed online at https://hbr.org/2020/04/4-things-sales-organizations-must-do-to-adapt-to-the-crisis.

[48] Gulati, Ranjay, et al. "Roaring Out of Recession," *Harvard Business Review* magazine, March 2010.

[49] "How 7 Firms Survived and Rebuilt after Crisis: Amazon, Sequoia Capital, Hostess, and Mpre," CB Research, 11 June 2020: Accessed online at https://www.cbinsights.com/research/business-strategies-survive-rebuild-crisis/.

[50] "Coronavirus: The Black Swan of 2020," Sequoia. 5 March 2020: Accessed online at https://medium.com/sequoia-capital/coronavirus-the-black-swan-of-2020-7c72bdeb9753.

[51] Benton, Jim, and Pete Kazanjy, "How Sales Teams Can Make the Most of Their Meetings and Sell to the C-Suite," The Weekly Briefing, Chorus, 27 August 2020.

[52] Goudreault, Jackie. "The Enterprise Motion: Navigating Complex Relationships," Chorus, 4 March 2021. Accessed online August 2021 at https://www.chorus.ai/blog/enterprise-motion-twb.

[53] Benton, Jim, and Pete Kazanjy, "How Sales Teams Can Make the Most of Their Meetings and Sell to the C-Suite." Chorus Weekly Briefing, 27 August 2020.

[54] Kafil, Mohammed, "Rethinking Procurement in the Post-Pandemic Era," PASA Thought Leadership, 12 August 2021. Accessed online at: https://procurementandsupply.com/2021/08/rethinking-procurement-in-the-post-pandemic-era/.

[55] Knights-Ward, Elizabeth. "A Four Pillar Framework for Sales and Marketing Alignment," LinkedIn Sales Blog. 27 August 2020. Accessed online at: https://www.linkedin.com/business/sales/blog/sales-and-marketing/a-four-pillar-framework-for-sales-and-marketing-alignment.

[56] "The Art of Winning: Orchestrating Sales and Marketing to Deliver the Ultimate Customer Experience," LinkedIn Sales Blog. 19 September 2018. Accessed online at: https://www.linkedin.com/business/sales/blog/sales-and-marketing/the-3-b2b-sales-and-marketing-structural-gaps-hampering-business.

[57] Grant, Adam. *Think Again*. Viking: 2021.

[58] Popik, Barry. "We Lose Money on Every Sale, But Make It Up On Volume." 25 February 2011. Accessed online at: https://www.barrypopik.com/index.php/new_york_city/entry/we_lose_money_on_every_sale_but_make_it_up_on_volume/.

[59] Pricing & Profitability: Deals Desk—A Key Business Enabler to Meet Customer Demands." PwC Technology Institute whitepaper. July 2014.

[60] Tim Riesterer, *Why Pay More eBook* (Reno, NV: Corporate Visions, 2021), eBook.

[61] Ramos, Laura. "Millennials Want Credible Digital Content -So Give It to Them!" Forrester blog. 19 February 2020. Accessed online at: https://www.forrester.com/blogs/millennials-want-credible-digital-content-so-give-it-to-them/.

62 Cohen, Rafi. "5 Ways to Create an Exceptional Customer Service Experience (& 4 Mistakes to Avoid," HubSpot, 24 January 2021, updated 15 June 2021. Accessed online September 2021 at https://blog.hubspot.com/service/customer-service-experience.

63 Bendersky, Ari. "How to Build Brand Trust, and Why It's the Ultimate Currency," The Salesforce 360 Blog. Accessed online at: https://www.salesforce.com/blog/how-to-build-brand-trust/.

64 Bages-Amat, Arnau, et al. "These Eight Charts Show How Covid-19 Has Changed B2B Sales Forever," McKinsey & Company blog, 14 October 2020. Accessed online September 2021 at McKinsey, https://www.mckinsey.com/business-functions/marketing-and-sales/our-insights/these-eight-charts-show-how-covid-19-has-changed-b2b-sales-forever.

65 Costet, Jonathan. "30 Mind-Blowing Sales Stats That Will Change The Way You Sell," Gong.io, 25 June 2021. Accessed online at: https://www.gong.io/blog/sales-stats/.

66 Renjen, Punit, "The Perseverance of Resilient Leadership: Sustaining Impact on the Road to Thrive," Deloitte Insights, 6 August 2020.

67 Benton, Jim, and Joel Rackham. "Selling to the C-Suite," Chorus *The Weekly Briefing* webinar. 17 September 2020.

68 Perrilleon, Rob, and Ryan Longfield. "Selling to the C-Suite: Learn How to Get a 'Yes' from Decision Makers," Gong.io webinar, episode 8: 9 April 2021.

69 Shallard, Paul. "The Need for Resilient and Transparent Supplier Relationships," Deloitte Consulting Blog, 10 May 2021. Accessed online at: https://www2.deloitte.com/nz/en/blog/consulting/2021/the-need-for-resilient-and-transparent-supplier-relationships.html.

70 "Key Trends Driving Change in the Next Era of E-Procurement," B2B E-Commerce in Evolution Report. Amazon Business. December 2020-January 2021.

71 "No More Excuses: The Time for B2B Digital Transformation Is Now," 2021 B2B Buyer Report. Avionos. February-March 2021.

72 Singer, Lisa. "Price: Not the Most Important Driver of B2B Buying Decisions." Forrester blog, 27 August 2015. Accessed online at: https://www.forrester.com/blogs/pricenotthemostimportant driverofbtobbuyingdecisions/. Updated information accessed online at: https://www.dnb.com/perspectives/marketing-sales/adapting-and-succeeding-in-changing-sales-environment-dnb-for-rester-webinar.html.

73 Greulich, Tim, and Laura Ramos, "Humanizing B2B Experiences," Deloitte Digital presentation, March 2021.

74 Riley, Craig, and Brent Adamson. "The Gartner Chief Sales Officer's Leadership Vision: Win in 2022." Gartner webinar. 18 October 2021.

75 Lai, Angali, et al. "The Trust Imperative: The Opportunities of Creating a Deliberate Trust Strategy and the Risks of Leaving It to Chance." Forrester Report. 12 May 2021. Accessed online at: https://www.forrester.com/report/The-Trust-Imperative/RES164983?objectid=RES164983.

76 *The State of Employee Mental Health in 2021*, Ginger, as referenced in press release dated 9 April 2020, accessed via Businesswire.

[77] Foster, Sarah. "55% of Americans Expect to Search for a New Job Over the Next 12 Months," Bankrate Personal Finance, 23 August 2021. Accessed online at: https://www.bankrate.com/personal-finance/job-seekers-survey-august-2021/.

[78] McClain, Mark. "Leaders: Get Ready for the Boomerang That's Coming After the Great Resignation," Fast Company, 09 November 2021.

[79] Chappuis, Bertil, et al. "The Domino Effect: How Sales Leaders Are Reinventing Go-to-Market in the Next Normal," McKinsey & Company, 1 October 2020. Accessed online at: https://www.mckinsey.com/business-functions/marketing-and-sales/our-insights/the-domino-effect-how-sales-leaders-are-reinventing-go-to-market-in-the-next-normal.

[80] Kelly, Bob, and Michelle Vazzana, "*Executing Hard Pivots in Sales Strategy*," Sales Management Association, 27 Oct. 2020. Accessed online at: https://salesmanagement.org/resource/research-first-look-executing-hard-pivots-in-sales-strategy/.

[81] McNeely, Robert. "7 Tips for Coaching Your Remote Sales Team," Revenue blog. 7 January 2018. Accessed online at: https://www.revenue.io/blog/7-tips-for-coaching-remote-sales-teams.

[82] Chappuis, Bertil, et al.

[83] Croswell, Lexi. "Focus on Learning and Development to Increase Retention." Culture Amp. Accessed online at: https://www.cultureamp.com/blog/focus-on-learning-development-to-increase-retention.

Extended Table of Contents

Made in the USA
Las Vegas, NV
17 June 2022

50305685R00122